35 UP

THE BOOK OF THE GRANADA TV SERIES

CLAIRE LEWIS AND KELLY DAVIS

NETWORK BOOKS

To those 14 people, their relatives and friends,
who have made this project possible.

ACKNOWLEDGEMENTS

We would like to thank Fiona Cosgrove for all her hard work and help in putting this book together. Also, thanks to Suzanne Webber, Nicky Copeland and Jennifer Jones for their editorial advice; to Ann Salisbury for her design work; to photographer Ged Murray; and to Michael Apted, Gordon McDougall, Paul Almond and Derek Granger for their memories and contributions. Last and not least, thanks to my husband, Ian White, and Kelly Davis's husband, Ian Francis, for their unfailing support, patience and understanding.

Network Books is an imprint of BBC Books,
a division of BBC Enterprises Limited,
Woodlands, 80 Wood Lane,
London W12 0TT

First published 1991
Compilation © Claire Lewis and Kelly Davis 1991

ISBN 0 563 36202 2

Set in 12/15pt ITC Garamond Light Condensed by
Ace Filmsetting Ltd, Frome, Somerset
Printed and bound in Great Britain by Clays Ltd, St Ives plc
Cover printed by Clays Ltd, St Ives plc

CONTENTS

FOREWORD

For all its influence and power, television rarely achieves the distinction of a programme that is lasting and unique. For most of the time our business is ephemeral; programmes live briefly both at transmission and in the memory. Once or twice they achieve glory, like our own *Brideshead Revisited* and *Jewel in the Crown*, before they pass into television folklore.

7–14–21–28–35 Up has, by comparison, a permanency in television history, an experience to be relived once every seven years and a reunion with characters whose lives we have watched develop from fantasy to reality – the nearest television gets to Shakespeare's seven ages. It is to the credit of those characters that we are allowed into their private worlds, and to the credit of Michael Apted and his production team to have won the trust that persuades them to confide in him for our interest and understanding.

David Plowright
Chairman, Granada Television

PICTURE CREDITS

Camera Press 16 (bottom), 17 (right), 19 (middle), 20 (left); Hulton Deutsch Collection 14 (top), 17 (left); Kobal Collection 19 (bottom); Courtesy the Pretty Ugly Agency 28, 29; Rex Features 18, 19 (top), 20 (right), 21; Syndication International 14 (bottom), 15, 16 (top).
Pictures of the 'children' at 35 taken by Ged Murray.
All other photos courtesy Granada Television and contributors.

INTRODUCTION

by Claire Lewis

The *Seven Up–28 Up* series has become a classic piece of television. *Seven Up* itself is one of the finest, most entertaining and enduring of all television documentaries. In retrospect, however, the programme's success is not surprising because it brought together a group of talented people, many of whom were to emerge as major forces in TV and film and theatre in the seventies and eighties.

Seven Up had a humble beginning. It was commissioned as a *World in Action* special, a one-off programme, at the end of the 1964 series. The *World in Action* of 1964 was raw, brash, investigative journalism – seeking out the truth, exposing corruption nationally and internationally, in a popular format. The original idea for *Seven Up* came from Australian *émigré* and former *Daily Express* editor Tim Hewat, then editor of *World in Action*. For some years Hewat had been fascinated by the maxim attributed to the Jesuits: 'Give me the child until he is seven and I will show you the man.'

Having been brought up as a Protestant, Tim Hewat was interested by the idea that your personality could be moulded and fixed by the age of seven. As an Australian, Hewat had been struck, when he first arrived in England to work on the *Daily Express*, by the rigidity of the English class system. What he did was to combine these two ideas, setting out to test the Jesuit theory in relation to social class in Britain in the mid sixties:

> I became convinced that the saying, 'Give me the child until he is seven and I will show you the man' was true. I became convinced that if you can control what someone thinks until they are seven that's the way they live their lives.

Tim Hewat, the founder and editor of *World in Action*.

The success of the original *Seven Up*, Hewat thinks, had a good deal to do with Canadian director Paul Almond, whom he brought in to direct the film, and with the selection of the children by the two researchers. Hewat says that Almond's incredible patience with the children was what helped make the programme so special. Soon after instigating *Seven Up*, Hewat left Granada and went back to Australia, where he now earns his living as a writer.

Lord Bernstein

So, in the spring of 1964, the idea of *Seven Up* was born. Gathered round Tim Hewat on *World in Action* were Derek Granger, later to become the producer of *Brideshead Revisited*; Sidney Bernstein, now Lord Bernstein and the founder of Granada Television, who always took a lively interest in *World in Action*; Cecil Bernstein, his brother; and Denis Forman, now Sir Denis Forman, former chairman of Granada. Hewat sold them his idea for a film on seven-year-old children and got the extra money needed for research.

He took on two young television researchers to start work on the programme, Michael Apted and Gordon McDougall. Both were Cambridge graduates who had just completed Granada's production trainee course early in 1964. Gordon McDougall remembers it well:

> That first day, Hewat outlined his idea. 'If I'm making this film,' said Hewat, 'my opening shot is an aerial camera on the top of Golden Square, shooting down the 20 seven-year-olds. 'Of these 20 kids,' I say, 'five are going to be winners' (zoom in) 'and 15 are going to be losers' (zoom in). 'Now we're going to show you why.'
>
> We supposed artists nodded condescendingly at this barbarian tabloid conceit and then went out and made a film which, though not in those words, said exactly that.

Michael Apted pays tribute to Tim Hewat as the architect of the film:

> I think he was the genius behind it all. To put the whole thing in a wider context, it was largely Hewat who reinvented current affairs and documentaries in the early sixties. He put tabloid journalism on television. Up till then it had been very establishment, very *Panorama*, very much the world of the BBC. His output was peppered with urgent and racy subject matter. It was blue collar television – noisy, vulgar, quick-witted and of the moment. *Seven Up* was some of the above, but it was the film-making of Paul Almond that gave it softer edges and a long life.

Derek Granger replaced Tim Hewat as executive producer of *World in Action* early on in *Seven Up*'s life, just as the work began on selecting children for the film. 'How did you choose the children?' is a question that has been asked of Michael Apted many times since 1964:

> I rang round the education departments in various boroughs and they recommended schools to me. We really didn't have much time so we were thankful for the help we received. When we got to a school we

would ask the form teacher to recommend the children they thought would be best in front of the camera, and we took over from there.

'We chose groups,' says Apted, 'because it gave us all sorts of mileage – it was more economic and allowed us to get more children into the film in a shorter screen time. In later years we were able to find out whether friendships formed at seven flourished or died on the vine. Reuniting people after years of separation became one of the signatures of the films, and it was fun to see those with identical backgrounds choosing different paths in their lives.'

After six weeks of intensive research, five times as much as a weekly *World in Action*, it was time to start filming. Paul Almond remembers how he coaxed a new style of shooting from cameraman David Samuelson:

> Little Tony would go running into the classroom. I said, 'Let's go running with him,' and it was, 'What do you mean?' It was in the early days of shooting, you know. 'What do you mean, run in with him? We haven't got a dolly, there are no grips, we can't . . .' I said, 'No, just take the camera and run with him.' And he was very put out at first, thought this was an atrocious idea, thought he'd probably get fired as soon as they saw the rushes. Anyway, I sort of jollied him up and he jumped in and squatted down and he ran with the little Cockney chap at his level. And that was of course how we wanted all the style of the film to be. In other words, a fluid camera, following the kids, hand-held. But it wasn't in the days of a steadicam, this was just a little Ari [Arriflex 16mm camera] that he held. We shot it silently, I think, and he just ran and that's how we were able to catch a lot of this.

Paul Almond,
the director of *Seven Up*.

On the final day of filming all the children were brought together for a day in London. They had a trip to the zoo, a visit to an adventure playground and a party. Says Gordon McDougall:

> It was wonderful to see them enjoying themselves, being children, but more than that, it was fascinating to see them together, to see all these separate entities we had researched and lived with, inter-reacting.

Paul Almond remembers it slightly differently:

> We thought this party would be such an exciting moment. We hired two more cameras, got our lights ready, got the table laid with food, napkins and balloons. I marshalled my troop of three cameras and felt like Cecil B. De Mille. The doors opened, the kids poured in and there

wasn't a sound. As soon as they saw the food they sat seriously down at their places, didn't utter a peep and munched slowly. The three cameras rolled away on absolutely nothing! It was very funny.

As executive producer, Derek Granger had to knock a two-and-a-half-hour roughcut into shape, and found cutting the children's comments – the 'talking head' portions of the film – very difficult. Says Granger:

> It is quite simply the best television documentary ever made. The overwhelming thing was that it reinforced the idea that we don't change. It shows that children are in fact people from a very early age and that they are extremely aware. The film gives you a shock when you see that awareness.

Gordon McDougall,
researcher on *Seven Up*.

Gordon McDougall says of *Seven Up*:

> The show was first transmitted on 5 May 1964, having been four months in the making. Normal *World in Action*s were conceived at the Tuesday morning conference and transmitted the following Monday. We never heard from Hewat whether he thought the investment was worth it or whether we came anywhere near his vision.
>
> For me *Seven Up* changed my view of society. I had always believed we lived in a land of flawed but real opportunity and I had rapidly to accept that my own findings proved conclusively this was not so. I know that there are many hurt feelings across the country as a result of our interference in people's lives. But I believe that what has been achieved is a fascinating and invaluable document of the twentieth century, an incarnation of a brilliant idea and model for documentary-makers of the future.

What does Michael Apted think was the secret of the success of *Seven Up*?

> I think it brought the best out of us all. There was a particular tension between Paul Almond and myself at the editing stage which benefited the final product. He was most concerned with making a fluid, attractive documentary about the world of the seven-year-old and created some memorable sequences – the three East London girls on the morning walk to school, Tony charging over fences and Nick wandering through the Yorkshire Dales. I found this all slightly irritating as I thought he was missing the point. To me, the heart of the matter was the class conflict, the differences in opportunity, the unfairness of it all.

I remember being very intense about it, and Paul took from that, used what he wanted and created something better than either of us, on our own, might have made.

Michael Apted's career continued to progress at Granada. He remained in regional features and documentaries for a short time and then became holiday relief director on *Coronation Street*. This was his big break in drama. He was responsible for casting Lynne Perrie (still an important member of the cast) as Ivy Tilsley. He then directed a number of television plays, among them *Number 10* and *Mosedale Horseshoe*, before he became freelance.

In 1977, when Michael Apted returned again to see how his 'children' were at 21, his career had been transformed. He had moved from London to Los Angeles and he had made several feature films. His first, *Triple Echo*, starred Glenda Jackson and Oliver Reed; this was followed by *Stardust*, with David Essex, *The Squeeze*, and *Agatha*, with Dustin Hoffman and Vanessa Redgrave.

At 21 the transformation of the 'children' into adults was almost complete, and *21 Up* captures all the delightful arrogance and vitality of the young adult! Two of the girls were married, six of the 'children' were at university, the rest all working, except for one – and only one – who seemed not to have taken the path set out for him.

I started work on *28 Up* in June 1984 and there were one or two people who were very difficult to find. For example, Paul, who now lived in Australia, had gone missing. Then there was Neil, last heard of in a London squat in 1977, for whom we had no address. My overriding memories of the research in 1984 are of trying to find Neil and keep tabs on him long enough to be able to get a crew to film him. There was also my first trip to the States to interview Nick, now a nuclear physicist, and a look – if fleeting – at Australia's outback with Paul. But for me, as for millions of others, the enduring image of *28 Up* is the lonely figure of Neil by a beautiful Scottish loch.

In the eyes of the critics and the public, *28 Up* was the most successful film of the series. In 1985 it won the Flaherty Award for Documentary at BAFTA, an RTS award for the most original television programme, an International Emmy, and the Blue Ribbon at the Los Angeles Film Festival. It's been shown all over the world and every now and again one or other of the participants will receive a stack of letters from a country where *28 Up*, or indeed the series, has just been shown.

Steve Morrison, executive producer of *28 Up*, now director of programmes at Granada, says:

> *28 Up* reached parts of the audience other documentaries don't. Seeing these kids stretch into adults, with all their ambitions realised or dashed, struck a chord with viewers' own hopes and memories.
>
> *28 Up* attracted an audience of over 10 million – an astonishing figure for a late evening transmission. We didn't realise the nerve we had touched. The day after we were deluged with newspaper demands for interviews with our participants. We were amazed.
>
> I have never been involved with any documentary that created such an impact.

Everyone who has taken part in *Seven Up*, *Seven Plus Seven*, *21 Up* and *28 Up* has been asked to participate in the writing of this book, which has been a collaboration between all of them, Kelly Davis and myself. The chapters are all slightly different in format, reflecting various people's involvement. We have published, unchanged, what they have written – and there are some very different personal views recorded. Only two of the 14 did not want to participate at all.

It has been a great privilege to work with everyone on the book and the series, and I would like to thank them all for their patience and good humour under what have sometimes been difficult circumstances.

The final day's filming of *Seven Up* at an adventure playground.

FROM *SEVEN UP* TO *35 UP*

by Michael Apted

I was in the Granada canteen with Jack Rosenthal one day in 1970 talking over a comedy series we were doing together, *The Lovers*, when Denis Forman joined us. 'It's nearly seven years since *Seven Up*,' he said. 'Wouldn't it be a nice idea to go and see how the children are doing now?' I said that I thought it might, so as casually as that I re-embarked on a project that has engaged my entire working life.

Michael Apted.

I've known the subjects of these films for over 25 years. The sheer longevity of the project has, I think, made it unique in the history of the medium, but back in the days of *Seven Plus Seven* such resilience seemed improbable. The interviews were like pulling teeth (they lacked, you might say, a warm glow), but once David Naden had edited it all together we knew we were on to something. The politics of the original were as strong as ever, but now we had the excitement of counterpointing two generations, of seeing people start to grow up. We had turned a page in the family album.

I had reduced the original group of 20 to a more manageable 14, but in doing so had compounded a felony that was going to haunt me as long as the series survived – the lack of women. There are no excuses. Choosing only four girls was bad planning and it meant we missed out on the women's movement, one of the most powerful social and political upheavals of my lifetime. I tried to patch it up by introducing spouses into the cast, but it's a gap I regret.

Be that as it may, it's still a minefield of problems to be navigated, as we learned in 1977 with *21 Up*. We had begun to accumulate a large amount of footage on each person over the three generations – the awkwardness of 14 had evaporated and interviewing had become much easier. I was having to condense a life into 15 or so minutes and make value judgements as to what was important and what wasn't.

Sometimes I was way off – Tony, for example. I felt he'd never had a real chance in life – high spirits and a quick wit weren't going to be enough. So I filmed him driving around the hot crime spots of the East End in his taxi-cab, giving a conducted tour of highlights past and present. I suppose I was planning ahead, second-guessing what was lying in wait for him, but I had misjudged him completely. As Tony would often say to me, 'Michael, you can't judge a book by its cover!' The wildness of his early years had softened and the energy was channelled into his marriage and children. His roots became a real source of strength and by 20 he'd really begun to make something of himself.

Our process is hardly scientific, more a complicated and sometimes bewildering array of private moments set against the cultural and social background of the times. Every seven years I do an exhaustive interview with each person, with very little preparation, looking for the spontaneous rather than the prepared response. We use a fraction of what we shoot (30 to 1) so we stockpile an enormous amount of film. With each generation of the series we start from scratch, and sometimes go back into unused interview footage if it has unexpectedly become relevant. It's a killer, how little time we have to tell so much and we rarely have the room to do people justice.

By 1984 and *28 Up* I think the series had changed dramatically – the politics were now unspoken and the class distinctions self-evident. The individual drama moved to the foreground and the human element began to dominate. I took the film to America, seriously doubting that anybody would make head or tail of it unless they were well versed in our school and class system, but I was wrong. It found a huge audience of people who were responding not to a thinly disguised political polemic, but to something universal. Success, failure, promise and disappointment – these had become the new currency of the film. Images would stay in the mind: Neil hitchhiking forlornly around Scotland; Suzy blossoming into motherhood, both belying what we thought might happen to them; Bruce teaching Bengali children, the ambition of a seven-year-old realised; Tony, alone with his jockey pictures, a dream abandoned.

I doubt that *28 Up* achieved the magical quality of the original – maybe that's the prerogative of seven-year-old children – but it had power and resonance. To the pimply shyness of 14 and the gamecock maturity of 21 had been added sturdier fowl. Commitments had been made at the workplace and at home, the decisions we all have to make at some time or another. This is what caught the audience's imagination, making it possible to identify with and relate to the people in the film. The way the public seemed to know the piece and talk about it was as gratifying to me as anything in my professional life; *28 Up* became personal to an audience in a way that's quite rare, and, for a time, I think it entered the culture – it was on the street.

Of course, there was a price to pay and the people in the film were the losers. For them the whole enterprise had become a colossal invasion of privacy. Two backed out at 28 and the major difficulty of mounting *35 Up* has been to hold in as many as possible. Inevitably it weakens the piece if it doesn't have a full cast – you lose the contrasts and comparisons, and miss people you feel you've grown up with.

For those who've stayed, there's a feeling of an extended family and some of us have got very close, although I'm sure they all dread the seven-yearly knock at the door. I'm extremely grateful to them for their patience and loyalty. Unfortunately there are a couple of them who are furious about the whole thing, who say they were sandbagged into it by parents and teachers, who feel their private embarrassment becomes public property every seven years. I'm sorry about it, but the films are too valuable just to abandon, and while I'm sure I've been guilty of a couple of cheap shots over the five films, I've never wilfully set out to misrepresent anybody or distort the truth.

I believe my greatest contribution to the whole project has been to hang in and give it continuity. I remember sitting with Mike Scott, then programme controller, in Los Angeles and saying wasn't it about time for *28*, and him telling me that it would never happen because I wouldn't leave my Hollywood career and go back and do it. He couldn't guess the power the films have in my life and how I doubt whether I'll ever have the chance to do anything as important as this again; important, for in a unique way you get a glimpse of the drama of what makes people who they are.

And there's yet another level in all this for me – the collaboration and friendship of the people I've grown up with making the series: Claire Lewis, my research associate and now series editor, and her predecessor, Margaret Bottomley; Mr and Mrs George Turner, cameraman and production assistant respectively (George has been an inspiration to me for three of the films); Nick Steer on sound and Kim Horton and the phalanx of editors, and not least, the management of Granada Television, whose support and backing over the years has guaranteed the very existence of the films. Thank you for that, and to everybody in this book – it's been an honour to be part of it all.

THAT WAS THE YEAR WHEN...
1964

Seven Up was shown on 5 May 1964.

JANUARY

Trend-setting British clothes designer Mary Quant attacked Paris fashion as out of date.

FEBRUARY

The Beatles flew from London to New York to find themselves mobbed by American fans.

MARCH

Ten of the Great Train Robbers were convicted.

The Beatles leaving London to start their American tour.

APRIL

Ian Smith became Prime Minister of Southern Rhodesia.

MAY

Fighting broke out between Mods and Rockers at Margate on the south coast.

JUNE

Nelson Mandela began his life sentence in the high-security prison on Robben Island.

Violence between Mods and Rockers leads to many arrests.

JULY

The Beatles' first film, *A Hard Day's Night*, had its London premiere.

AUGUST

President Johnson ordered a retaliatory air strike on the North Vietnamese coastline.

SEPTEMBER

In England, the *Daily Herald* newspaper was replaced by the *Sun*.

OCTOBER

Labour won the British general election, ousting the Tories after 13 years.

NOVEMBER

Lyndon Johnson was re-elected as US President.

The new prime minister, Harold Wilson, at the door of 10 Downing Street.

Ronnie (*left*) and Reggie Kray.

DECEMBER

In the East End of London, the Kray brothers were implicated in a shooting incident.

POP HITS

'I Love You Because'

THEATRE HITS

Laurence Olivier in *Othello*

TV HITS

Steptoe and Son

1970

Seven Plus Seven was shown on 15 December 1970.

JANUARY

Mick Jagger stood trial for possession of cannabis.

FEBRUARY

British writer and philosopher Bertrand Russell died, aged 97.

Mick Jagger and
Marianne Faithfull arriving at court.

MARCH

Eighteen children who suffered birth defects due to thalidomide were awarded nearly £370,000 in damages.

APRIL

US President Nixon ordered troops to attack Communist bases in Cambodia.

MAY

Six anti-Vietnam student demonstrators were shot dead at American universities.

JUNE

The Tories, led by Edward Heath, defeated Harold Wilson's Labour government in the general election.

Anti-Vietnam demonstrators outside the White House.

The British Army in the Falls Road in Belfast.

JULY

The sex musical *Oh! Calcutta!* opened at the Round House in London.

AUGUST

The British Army started using rubber bullets in Belfast.

SEPTEMBER

American rock star Jimi Hendrix died of a drug overdose, aged 28.

OCTOBER

Oil was struck for the first time in the British sector of the North Sea.

NOVEMBER

In France, thousands mourned the death of Charles de Gaulle.

Legendary guitarist Jimi Hendrix.

DECEMBER

Paul McCartney began legal proceedings against his fellow Beatles, John, George and Ringo.

POP HITS

'In the Summertime'

TV HITS

Monty Python's Flying Circus

FILM HITS

M*A*S*H

1977

21 Up was shown on 9 May 1977.

JANUARY

Gary Gilmore, the murderer who wanted to die, was executed in the USA.

FEBRUARY

Ugandan dictator Idi Amin had at least 130 of his opponents killed, including the Archbishop of Uganda.

The Pompidou Arts Centre opened in Paris, sparking controversy over its unusual design.

MARCH

574 people died when two jumbo jets collided on a runway in the Canary Islands.

APRIL

In London, there was fighting between National Front supporters and anti-Fascists.

National Front supporters marching in London.

MAY

Menachem Begin's right-wing Likud Party took power in Israel.

JUNE

Top jockey Lester Piggott won the Derby for the eighth time.

JULY

In Pakistan, Prime Minister Bhutto was ousted by General Zia.

AUGUST

Elvis Presley died, aged 42, at Graceland, his Memphis mansion.

SEPTEMBER

American film director Roman Polanski was jailed for having sex with a minor.

Freddie Laker's first Skytrain flight left Gatwick for New York.

OCTOBER

Police appealed to the public for information to help them find the Yorkshire Ripper.

'The King', Elvis Presley.

NOVEMBER

In the north of England, 700 jobs were lost at the Swann Hunter shipyard.

DECEMBER

The boat people started leaving Communist-run South Vietnam.

John Travolta, the star of *Saturday Night Fever*.

Ninety-six boat people awaiting rescue.

POP HITS

'Don't Cry for Me, Argentina'

FILM HITS

Rocky, *Star Wars* and *Saturday Night Fever*

THEATRE HITS

Alan Ayckbourn's *Bedroom Farce*

1984

28 Up was shown over two nights on 21 and 22 November 1984.

JANUARY

Boy George was Britain's latest pop sensation.

FEBRUARY

Jayne Torvill and Christopher Dean won the Olympic Gold Medal at Sarajevo.

Trend-setter Boy George.

Jayne Torville and Christopher Dean, World Champion ice-dancers.

MARCH

Foreign Office clerk Sarah Tisdall was jailed for six months for contravening the Official Secrets Act.

APRIL

American singer Marvin Gaye was shot dead by his father.

WPC Yvonne Fletcher was shot dead during the Libyan Embassy siege in London.

MAY

National Union of Miners leader Arthur Scargill was arrested in South Yorkshire during the miners' strike.

JUNE

Indian troops expelled Sikh extremists from the Golden Temple at Amritsar.

JULY

Twenty people were shot dead by a rampaging gunman in a Californian McDonald's restaurant.

AUGUST

The BMX bike craze arrived in Britain from the US.

SEPTEMBER

Twenty people died when the US Embassy in Beirut was attacked by a suicide bomber.

OCTOBER

An IRA bomb exploded at the Grand Hotel, Brighton, headquarters of the Tory Party Conference, killing three people and injuring more than 30.

The Grand Hotel in Brighton, following the explosion of an IRA bomb.

NOVEMBER

US President Reagan won a landslide electoral victory against Walter Mondale.

DECEMBER

2,000 people died and thousands more were blinded when poisonous gas leaked from a chemical factory in Bhopal, India.

Ex-film actor Ronald Reagan, the president of the United States.

POP HITS

'Do They Know It's Christmas?' and Michael Jackson's *Thriller* album

FILM HITS

Amadeus

TV HITS

The Jewel in the Crown

TONY

‘I wanna be a jockey when I grow up. Yeah, I wanna be a jockey. ’

I was born in Bethnal Green Hospital in the East End. We lived in a two-up two-down terrace house till I was five, and I shared a bed with my two older brothers, Johnny and Joey. My mum used to wash us kids in a tin bath in front of the fire. Then we moved to a three-bedroomed flat in Waterloo Gardens and I shared a room with Johnny and Joey. My sister Brenda had her own room and blankets on her bed – we just had old coats and jackets.

Dad used to work as a porter in the meat market but he was caught nicking meat and had to do two years inside. I remember once asking Mum where he was and she said he was building huts for the Germans! His health was always dodgy; he lost a kidney when he was 12 and he used to get asthma. When he came out of prison he made his money gambling – he was a three-card trickster. If he had a win he used to buy us new plimsoles or baseball boots. Sometimes, when we was really skint, Mum used to take her iron over to the pawnshop. Once she took it when it was still hot from doing the ironing, and the pawnbroker complained! She was always at home to look after us kids. We got free school dinners and she cooked pie mash, bacon bone stew or whatever in the evening. I used to help in a local fruit shop when I was five or six. That was my first ever wage – they paid me half-a-crown a week.

There was 30 kids in our class at Mowlem Street Primary. I was always running about and climbing over things – over walls, up drainpipes – you name it I was climbing it. Me and my mates used to go over to Victoria Park, swim in the canal, play hide-and-seek, and make camps in the wood yard. Sometimes we'd climb over the wall behind the local shop, nick the bottles

Tony's mum.

from the yard, then take them round the front to get the deposit (threepence per bottle).

We'd often go to the pictures on Saturday mornings. On Sundays I went to Sunday School at the Mildmay Mission. All the kids used to line up for orange and a biscuit, and I'd go round twice, wearing some other kid's coat and standing on tiptoe.

Tony at 7, on fighting:
'Is it important to fight? Yes.'

Tony's father:
'I used to take him to the dogs with me when he was about seven . . . He'd never been in trouble or nothing like that. He was a good boy, Tony. He idolised his mother . . . And when he done that programme they all asked him what he wanted to be. He said, "I wanna be a jockey," and he kept his word.'

Tony, at 35:
'In my opinion, I had the best upbringing a kid could ever want. The poverty was there but I never knew what it was. I done everything what every other kid done. I would honestly say I had more than some of them. You know why? Because I had adventure . . . My friends, they were in bed at seven o'clock. I wasn't even indoors . . .'

Tony during the filming of *Seven Up*.

AT 14

6 If I knew I couldn't be a jockey I'd get out of the game – I wouldn't bother. **9**

I went to Daneford Secondary Modern in the East End, but I spent all my free time at Tommy Gosling's racing stables at Epsom, learning to ride and look after horses. After leaving school I was hoping to go and work for Tommy Gosling for good. I also had my own racing greyhound and paid Mum so much a week to feed it. My oldest brother Johnny was a docker. The next oldest, Joey, was eight years older than me and he used to be in the Merchant Navy. When he came back I remember he had £100 and he put all the money out on the kitchen table – we'd never seen that many notes before. He bought me a reversible suit in brown and black. My sister Brenda was working as a telephonist at the time.

I didn't go out much in the evenings. Sometimes I'd go dog racing, play snooker or whatever, but more often I'd just stay in and watch TV. I didn't read books and if I read a paper it was the *Daily Mirror* because that's the one my dad used to buy. By the time I was 14 I'd been to Austria. I thought it was all right but I wasn't too bothered about travel. I didn't have a girlfriend – I didn't want to get married, have children or nothing like that. I wasn't often in trouble at school, although one time I was called up in front of the headmaster for 'bullying a bigger boy'!

Tony in his school football kit.

Tony

Tony at 14, on rich people:
'They can get what they want, can't they? . . . They can just ask for money and get it, and they can buy what they want.'

On race:
'If they want to come to this country they come, don't they? There's too many of them here . . . Good old Enoch. He's all right . . . Put in a vote who wants 'em to go and who wants 'em to stay.'

On violence:
'Every time the police catch a skinhead doing vandalism they should just give him a beating and that's it – and put him in a cell.'

On health:
'No, I won't ever smoke or drink. 'Cos if you smoke and drink it ruins your health and your health comes first, doesn't it?'

Tony's father:
'When he was 14 I used to go and see him, give him a couple of quid, because in them days a couple of quid was a lot of money . . . When he was at home I used to go to the spielers, the clubs. And he used to wait at the bottom of the stairs and say to me, "Dad, have you won?" And I'd say, "Here's a pound or so." . . . What we had to do when we was young to bring a family up, everybody in London done. If they didn't thieve they'd get it some other way, don't worry.'

Tony at 35:

'I never gave being a jockey my best shot, if the truth's known . . . It was self-inflicted. I wasn't dedicated enough. I was a town boy – and that had a lot to do with it . . . Because you think you're clued-up. You've had an upbringing of the streets – the chewing gum type of walk and the slouch. And you get there, with all these local yokels, and you feel you know more . . .'

AT 21

Tony on Chateau Dias.

❝ Dogs, prices, girls, the Knowledge, roads, streets, squares, Mum and Dad, and love. That's all I understand and that's all I want to understand. ❞

I rode in three races but I didn't make it as a jockey. I had a photo-finish at Newbury for third place and my last professional ride was at Windsor. After that I was placing bets for the punters at Hackney Wick Greyhound Stadium three afternoons a week. When *21* was being screened in 1977 there was a guy from the City – a very big wheel. He called me into his office by the Stock Exchange and he laid it on the line. He wanted me to be a blue button, 'cos he'd seen me running round putting bets on at Hackney Wick. There's a similarity in that respect, but I felt that it wasn't for me. As it happened, my older brother Johnny was working as a cabbie, and Joey and me was both on the Knowledge – I had to go out on the bike every day and learn hundreds of routes round London.

In the evenings I used to go out to all the pubs and clubs. I was always a keen gambler but I never drank or smoked. On Sunday mornings I used to play football or help sell T-shirts from my mate's stall in Petticoat Lane. There was lots of birds around at the clubs but I didn't have a girlfriend at the time. Every year I used to go on holiday to Spain with a whole gang of mates. When I was 21 I was starting to get into the acting game – I'd already had a day's work as an extra on *The Sweeney*.'

I used to drive a G-reg Hunter. It was the apple of my eye, that car. I was still living at home, although we was about to leave the flat because Mum couldn't manage the stairs no more with her arthritis.

Tony at 21, on riding:

'All of a sudden when he says, ''Jockeys, please mount'', and the bell went ding ding, then my heart just sunk because I thought to myself, here I was yesterday, sort of nobody, and here I am today, I'm the king, right. I felt king for one day . . . I would've given my right arm at the time to become a jockey, but now, well I wasn't good enough – it's as easy as that.'

On becoming a taxi-driver:

'I want to prove any person who thinks I can't be a cab-driver wrong, and get that badge and put it right in their face, just to tell them how wrong they can be.'

On gambling:

'Some people drink and they can't get out of drinking. Some people smoke and they can't stop smoking. But I think I'm certainly on the ground with the gambling. I know you can't win gambling, putting money on the dogs and horses, I know that, but when you put other people's money on, well you can't lose.'

On being short:

'A bird said to me the other day, she said, ''Ain't you small?'' So I said, ''But you're ugly. At least I can grow.'' '

On girls:

'You understand the four Fs? Find 'em, feed 'em, forget 'em – for the other F I'll let you use your own discretion. I mean, this one. I tried to do the three Fs but I couldn't forget her . . . It sounds silly, but it's the only way I could put it.'

On living in the East End:

'I wouldn't want to get out, really. It's very hard to make it in the East End, I've got my roots firmly stuck in the ground and I'd have a big hard pull to get 'em out.'

On crime:

'How can I become a villain? If it's not in me, if it's not born in me, how can I become one?'

On education:

'There's no education in this world – it's just one big rat race and you've got to kill the man next to you to get in front of him.'

On his ambition:

'There's only one ambition I want, really. I want a baby son, and if I see my baby son, that's my ambition fulfilled.'

On himself:

'I don't want to change, because if I change it proves the other Tony Walker was all fake.'

Tony's father:

'I felt proud seeing him ride. I took my missus, my other boys come with me, and we went to Newbury, Kempton, Windsor . . . But you give yourself two years in that game – he had three. Once he couldn't make it, times were very hard . . . So when he came out he went on the Knowledge and he passed the Knowledge . . . You can never be skint when you're a cab-driver. No matter what you do – you can gamble – but you're never skint. All you gotta do is get behind the wheel.'

Tony at 21.

Tony at 35:

'If it hadn't been for my brother Johnny I would've been a villain.'

AT 28

 It's just the way I'm made. I'm a happy-go-lucky type of fella, typical East Ender, which the attitude is hello mate how are you type of thing. I wouldn't want to lose that.

By 28 I was married to my Debbie. We met in a pub where she used to work behind the bar on Friday nights. Then we met again in a disco and I was like a bee round honey – she couldn't get rid of me! When they made *28 Up* we had two kids – Nicky was nearly seven, and my Jodie was two and a half – and we was living in a downstairs council flat in a terrace house in Islington,

round the corner from Debbie's mum and brothers. My parents was living in sheltered housing in Bethnal Green and Mum was still lively even with the arthritis. If there was seven days in the week we was up there five days. My mum, without a doubt, best woman in the world with respect to Debbie.

I was working nights driving the taxi and Debbie was keeping the books. If we couldn't afford to pay a bill I'd just stay out in the cab till I'd earned enough to pay it. Debbie drove a little Ford Fiesta at the time. We was eating well and buying nice clothes for ourselves and the kids. We had a caravan at Canvey Island (about an hour away), where Debbie used to take Nicky and Jodie most weekends. Debbie wasn't going out to work then. She was looking after the kids most of the time, and she was expecting the third. Nicky and Jodie was signed up with a children's modelling agency and they'd done a few ads.

I wasn't riding much any more – just the odd weekend canter at Epsom – but I was playing a lot of golf. I'd joined two golf societies, playing different courses all year round, and I won a number of trophies. Most of my golfing mates were publicans or cabbies, but we used to get some snooty types at some of the golf clubs. I was also doing quite a bit of acting, getting work as a film extra and taking acting lessons.

At 28 I was thinking about buying my own pub. I thought I'd like to be a publican – if it didn't work out I knew I could always go back to driving a cab.

Tony in his taxi.

Tony at 28, on being a taxi-driver:
'I love being a taxi-driver. I like the outdoor life, the independence, there's no
one to govern me, to say like you've gotta be in at a certain time.'

On riding:
'My greatest fulfilment in life was when I rode at Kempton in the same race
as Lester Piggott . . . All my years from seven, all my ambition fulfilled in one
moment. When the long feller come out, and I'm in with him like in the
same room . . . Money in the whole world couldn't buy that . . . I eventually
finished last. Tailed off, obviously. But it didn't make any difference to me.
Just to be part of it. Be with the man himself . . . That was the proudest day
of my whole life.'

On acting:
'I like it. I mean I think to myself I can do that. I still wanna have a go at it.
I mean nothing for fame and fortune . . . Hollywood and bright lights – it's
nothing like that. Just a sideline.'

On himself:
'I like to feel that I don't want to keep still. 'Cos life don't wait for nobody, so
you got to cram it in as much as you can before your days are numbered.'

'I can judge people on what they are rather than who they are.'

Tony

On education:
'When I said there's no education . . . I made a great mistake in saying that.
But I didn't mean to say there's no education as far as academically. Yes,
there is. The area, the environment, the education makes a person have more
opportunities in this world . . . That's obvious.'

On the other children featured in 7 Up:
'Being in a prep school they're missing the love and the care what every East
Ender gets.'

On being a father:
'When my kids are growing up I wanna see the change in them all the time,
so I have my own memories of when they was a kid and how they were.'

'Now I'm in a position . . . through my job, you know, to give my kids the
life I never had . . .'

Tony's father:

'My boys were brought up not to do anything wrong. But you know what it's like with children. You can't be at the back of them all the time. But they turned out all right. Every one's their own guv'nor. They all drive cabs – even my daughter drives a black cab – and they ain't done too bad now, have they?'

The most important thing that's happened to me in the last few years was the death of my mum. We were exceptionally close. She was like a goddess to all the kids, the backbone of the whole family. And she was a great conjuror with money. Even on her deathbed, when she had six or seven hours to go, she got my sister Brenda and whispered to her, 'Bandages, bandages.' She died holding our hands. And then next day Brenda said, 'I gotta go upstairs before me dad gets there.' She went straight to the tin, unrolled the crêpe bandages, and there was £20, there was £50, like a toilet roll full of money. And that was Mother – cunning as a fox.

At her funeral, various cab-drivers turned up. And we're going along, the family car, the friends' car, the hearse, and all the cabs, when someone cuts in. Out of respect the golden rule in the East End is that if you see a funeral procession you don't overtake and most of all you don't cut in. So this guy cuts in. One of the cab-drivers – he's a lovely man but he's very short-fused – he done no more than stop his cab . . . which held up the whole of Bethnal Green. Then he's pulled the other driver out by the scruff of his neck and they start fighting in the middle of the road. It could only happen on my mother's funeral!

She was a very unique woman, my mum. Debbie's very like her – the affectionate side, the lovable side, the generosity side. I say a prayer for Mother every night, and we go and visit her grave on birthdays and Christmas days.

Dad never really got over Mother's death – I mean, they was together for 45 years. But after she died he lived his life gambling. He was around with all the boys, he was playing cards and he loved the betting shop. He gave me his card and he used to say, 'If ever you want me, Tony, I'm in there.' At the front there was a takeaway snackbar, but behind there was a card school. He was so nonchalant. I'd say, 'You're never in when I phone you, Dad.' And he'd say, 'Here's my card – I'll be at my club.'

He died very suddenly a few weeks ago. I was filming a programme at the BBC when Debbie arrived and told me Dad had collapsed. When I got to the hospital he was in intensive care and he never regained consciousness. I held one hand and Joey held the other, just like we did when Mother died. While he was lying in the chapel I put two packs of cards, three betting slips and some dice in the coffin.

Since he died, for the first time I've looked in the mirror and realised I've actually grown up. Anything I wanted to discuss, any precarious situation, I always used to ask the old man. They was everything to me, my mum and dad.

Losing your parents – I suppose that's a sign of the years going by and it makes you think about your own life. I feel I've achieved as much as I can in the taxi business, and I only wish I could get on more in the film game. I did try running a pub for a while but it wasn't for me.

I live in Islington in a three-bedroomed estate house, I run a cab and a car (a Fiat Uno), I've got three lovely kids and I'm married to my Debbie. We have our ups and downs like every couple. We row tooth and nail sometimes but at the end of the day I don't think there's any other girl for me.

Debbie drives a cab too. They done the Knowledge together, my wife and my sister, and there's now about 50 women taxi-drivers in Islington. They treat it like a social club! From one o'clock till two they'll stop at Harrods and have a cup of tea and a sandwich in the cafe. Then they go and look around the shop. They have the morning's takings, so they buy a nice little bag, see a T-shirt for the kids or whatever.

Tony at 35.

I drive the cab at night and Debbie does four hours a day but it isn't a question of passing ships in the night. I always have dinner with the family. She tells me her day events, I tell her my night events. If we want to go out together we just don't go to work. She appreciates me more now, knowing I've got to do a ten-hour shift.

My eldest kid, Nicky, he's gone through that stage where everything's stopped being roses. Whether it's the bullying, whether it's the gangs . . . whatever it may be. If I tell him to do something he'll have a little moan but at the end of the day he knows where it lies. When you've got children your responsibilities actually hit home. Nicky's 13 now. He's quite tall, taller than me. Not that I'm anything to go on!

Then there's Jodie who's coming on to nine. I'd say she's the most like me – very can't-wait-gotta-go, very chatterbox, very energetic. She swings and climbs to the highest height. And she's very caring, my Jodie, very soft-hearted. Very easy to affect if you say the wrong thing to her. The youngest one, Perri, is nearly five. She's at a private nursery, which we have to pay £20 a week to have her there. When she's five she'll go to the same primary school as Jodie.

I still have a bet on the horses. Everyone must have a vice, and I don't drink or smoke. There are pitfalls in gambling, but in my case I earn my money and every night I come home and I put it in the jar. Every morning I wake up and there's £10 left in that jar. Debbie's got to understand, whatever I earn I put it in, she takes it out and leaves me £10 a day. And that's for me.

I play golf, as in once a month, or once a week, time permitting. I've been in the Sunday Club for about nine years now, and I play abroad once a year. It's a great game, great social life. I'm still playing football too.

I haven't missed a Derby since '69, other than this year. But I would love to have been a jockey. And even now, I mean it tears you inside to see 'em. The bells – ding ding you know – you're ready to go. I still watch the horse racing every day. All my life – part of my life.

Tony with his wife Debbie and their three children
(*from left to right*) Nicky, Perri and Jodie.

BRUCE

‘ My heart's desire is to see my daddy who is 6,000 miles away. **’**

I lived in Rhodesia until I was about five. I remember being there – especially the spaces of the bush and a native village near our house. One afternoon I went missing; I was found hours later in the chapel with native Africans singing hymns.

At first my father managed a country club and then he became a civil servant. He was about 15 years older than my mother and had been married before. My parents separated when I was three or four, then they got divorced and I came back to England with my mother.

I was sent to Melbreck School in Hampshire when I was five. I wasn't just packed off – my mother had to work and if I'd said I didn't like it they'd have found something else. On the programme it looked fairly strict – those photographs of us lining up and doing drill – but I suppose everyone was acting a role. That one boy was being a sort of sergeant-major and we were all acting as recruits. I don't remember finding it particularly awful. If you behaved yourself and so on you got on very well.

The school was run by a family – a gentleman and his wife and their two daughters. There were about 30 pupils altogether, and maybe a dozen in each class. At seven, I remember our education was very competitive. We would be in order of desks, so that if you were in the top desk you were the brightest in the class. Occasionally the teacher would say, 'Right, well, I think you two better swap now. I think you're now brighter than he is.' I mean, I was always quite bright and fairly near the front. I don't know what effect it would have had on somebody who was stuck at the back. The teachers were kindly but sometimes I was naughty so I was beaten a few times, probably

Bruce at seven.

Bruce during the
filming of *Seven Up*.

with a slipper. But we always got on afterwards so it can't have been that
unfair at the time.

I do remember missing my father – he was a sort of figure in my
imagination – although he came over to England about once every two years.
We couldn't go home for weekends but occasionally our parents would come
down and visit us on a Sunday. They were times when you couldn't
completely let go because you'd still have to be in your uniform. They'd
organise a treat – like going to the sea – so they were nice days but it was all
a bit formal somehow.

In the holidays I'd go to my mother's flat in Harrow. She was working on
a magazine called *Coming Events in Britain,* and she sometimes had to go
on trips to places like Edinburgh and stay away from London for a couple of
nights. At times like that I'd stay with one of my aunts. Auntie Pam and
Auntie Margaret, my mother's older sisters, never had any children of their
own and they were always very nice to me. My grandparents lived next door
to our flat so we were all very close.

The flat had two bedrooms and it was in a private sixties block at the end
of a cul de sac. There was a bit of open ground where I used to play football
with some of the local boys. One of my friends from school also lived in
London and I'd occasionally see him in the holidays if we could fix it up.
When I wasn't playing football I always enjoyed reading, especially the C.S.
Lewis 'Narnia' books.

Bruce at 7, on religion:
'I think the most important thing in the world is that everyone should know
about God.'

On wanting to be a missionary:
'Well, I'll go into Africa and try and teach people who are not civilised to be
more or less good.'

On money:
'I think we should give all, some, most of our money to the poor people.'

On girls:
'Well, my girlfriend is in Africa and . . . I don't think I'll have another chance
of seeing her again, and there were two in Switzerland which I liked too, in
the . . . Park Hotel.'

Bruce's mother:

'The school was a good school but I was a bit sad that I had to send him to boarding school so young. It was very difficult. I was on my own and I was working. It was just very unfortunate.'

Bruce at 35:

'I remember saying at 28 that I'd been unhappy at Melbreck and I think that was probably true . . . But, I mean, everybody cries at some stage when they're young, and I don't think that was necessarily due to the fact that I was there . . .'

6 I don't want to be a missionary because I just can't talk about it to people. I am interested in it myself, but . . . I'm just not very good at . . . standing up in front of people and making a speech, or anything like that. I'd like to keep it private. 9

At 14 I was in my second year at St Paul's. I enjoyed it much more than my prep school. We had a far more adult relationship with the teachers. We'd sit in their rooms and talk about, you know, anything. My housemaster, Mr Perry, was a big influence because he took such an interest in us growing up, and I appreciated his guidance.

I went to St Paul's Junior School from eight to about 12. Then from 12 onwards I was at the senior school as a boarder. I always enjoyed maths and I suppose I was quite good at science, but I found Classics hard and I probably wasn't very good at English. At that time I apparently wanted to be a doctor but I don't really remember why. I found dissections and things like that very difficult – maybe I was just squeamish. Later on I decided to drop biology and do double maths at A-level.

Academically, we worked quite hard and St Paul's was a school where you had to be quite bright to get in, so there was a sort of hot-house atmosphere. But we were given a lot of freedom: for example, at weekends we could go out in the evenings or go shopping or anything.

Bruce at 14.

My mother remarried when I was eight or nine and my sister Sophie was born a year or two later. When I was about 12 I remember taking Sophie for a walk and she suddenly vanished in the lake. I yanked her out from the bank. I mean, I was responsible. She'd been silly but, you know, she was only two.

My stepfather was a writer – mainly history and some art books – and he also did some general editing work. We got on very well. I remember getting involved in the discussions he had with his friends. One was a scientist who had set up a sort of early environmental research centre in Wales, building houses with solar panels on the roof and all that sort of thing. We'd go there for holidays, and I remember being very interested in all this adult discourse. My stepfather and I used to have discussions on a very equal basis. I know he was a bit worried about me at one point. He was concerned that I seemed to be coping too well with having a new father. I wasn't showing any of the symptoms. You know, some kids become withdrawn or get upset very easily.

My mother and stepfather bought a house in the village of Deddington in Oxfordshire. At first we'd go there for the odd weekend but then my mother gave up her job and we eventually moved out there.

The village was a bit divided. There was a big main road and on one side there was a council estate, and on the other side there were Cotswold-type houses. At our end of the village there was a big playing field where kids used to go and kick a ball round. I remember having a few friends – I used to play for the village football team and so on – but I never formed any really long-lasting friendships there. I'd never gone to the local school with the local kids. At boarding school you just have to get on with people and there's always someone around, but in the village – perhaps it wasn't only that I was a bit different – I might also just not have had the knack of making friends.

As Deddington was only 70 or 80 miles from St Paul's it was quite manageable for weekends. Sometimes I had schoolfriends home for the weekend, if they fancied a change from going home or their parents lived abroad. I do remember the weekends being much more enjoyable than when I was at my first school. In the village it tended to be mainly boys playing football. We didn't mix much with the girls, and I remember feeling acutely embarrassed about girls at that age.

When I was 14 I went out to Rhodesia to see my father. I stayed for about a month and he organised wonderful treats for me – seeing game on safari, visiting Mozambique, and so on – although these treats somehow didn't seem to be part of Rhodesia. I had some awareness of the political situation there at the time. I remember going into a shop and the chap said to me, 'Well, look, you come up and be served first.' And I was saying, 'No, no, there's a queue here. I'm perfectly happy here.' But everybody else in front of me was not white, and they were terribly embarrassed that I was queueing behind them. It was little things like that – there was an attitude.

When I met my father again there was bit of distance between us. I suppose my father had sort of faded away and my stepfather was the one who was there while I was growing up.

Bruce at 14, on his senior school:

'At St Paul's I like the companionship, you know, with other boys . . . They don't sort of enforce being upper-class and things like that . . . They suggest that you don't have long hair and . . . they teach you to be reasonably well-mannered.'

On poverty:

'[I don't know much about poor people] because at school I'm always surrounded by people who are about the same class as me, in fact a bit higher . . . They're not poor in any way.'

On politics:

'I didn't agree with the Conservatives about what they were doing with the black people, you know, racial policy . . . None of the parties really seem to agree with me. I think if I had voted I'd have voted Labour.'

Bruce during the filming of *Seven Plus Seven*.

On student demonstrations:

'Demonstrations are all right, as long as they don't get violent. But it seems a bit stupid to demonstrate for peace when you go around creating battles and wars and breaking up places.'

On discipline:

'It would just be absolute chaos if you had no rules at all, but you know . . . if you go from a very strict rule into just a free world you'd just find the change so great you might not be able to cope with it . . .'

On religion:
'I mean . . . all the scientists said, "We've looked up into space and we haven't seen God so there isn't a God," and it just seems fatuous.'

On money:
'I don't think money means everything. If I was rich, for instance . . . I'd help people if I had a chance, you know, by say giving money to charity or sponsoring things . . .'

On television:
'I used to watch it a lot but I'm not watching it so much now. I think . . . a lot of it is corrupting me a bit . . . For one thing, the advertisements, you know. I can recite about six tunes off, and it just seems a worthless thing to know.'

On travel:
'Well, I ski in Switzerland and I enjoy that immensely. And we went to France this time and I've lived in Rhodesia.'

On sport:
'I think it's much better if you have a team, because you're all together . . . and it doesn't really matter if you lose or win because it's not really your fault, it's the team as a whole . . . I used to be quite a bad sportsman and whenever I lost I used to get very angry, but then I realised how I was sort of imposing on other people . . . and then I got a bit better at it. But you've also got to win well and not jeer, if you happen to win very easily.'

On girls:
'[I don't have a girlfriend] yet. I'm sure it will come, but not yet.'

Bruce's mother:
'He didn't get into the drugs scene when he was a teenager. That was the biggest worry in those days. It was the sixties and the drugs scene was very big.'

Bruce at 35:
'I know that my parents split up, but I find it difficult to form relationships anyway. I'd prefer to say, well that's something I've got to deal with now, rather than keep looking back for a particular excuse or reason.'

‘Melbreck probably had a great influence on me in a way. I mean, I was absolutely shocked rigid when I went to my prep school and found that people thought of doing things wrong. I never really upset anyone or questioned authority or misbehaved in any of my two later schools, which may seem an ideal sort of thing. But I think it's probably healthy to question why you have to do certain things, which I never did. ,

Bruce at 21.

I took nine months off between school and university, worked at Banbury sewage works for a few months and taught at a school for spastics. It was almost an accident that I ended up at that school but I'm glad I did it. I enjoyed it, not so much because of the slightly charitable nature of the work but because I got on quite well with the people and found the work interesting.

After that I went to University College, Oxford, to read Maths. At 21 I was in my final year and I realised I was struggling. I hadn't done much work in my second year so I had a lot to do to catch up. I enjoyed the maths course but I did find it difficult and I didn't work very hard. I eventually got a third-class degree.

I went to church regularly while I was at Oxford but I didn't get involved with any of the Christian groups. I had quite a good social life – meeting friends in pubs, going to concerts, seeing films and student theatre productions, playing football for the college team. The friends I made there have actually remained my closest friends. As for relationships, there weren't really that many women at Oxford at the time. A lot of the colleges were still men only. I mean, it wasn't actually difficult meeting somebody but that's different from getting involved. It just seemed to be a difficult process. In some ways I probably found it easier to form friendships with girls, just being, you know, companionable. Perhaps I found it more difficult because I'd always gone to boys' schools and then a male-only college. Some of my friends obviously had girlfriends. I don't know whether I was jealous or vicariously pleased for them. I think it was just something I still had to tackle.

In the holidays I usually stayed with my mother and stepfather in Deddington. Sophie went to a local school in Oxfordshire and then she went to Oxford High, a girls' grammar. We were always very pleased to see each other when I came home from university. I also went on a few trips. I remember going to Vienna and to a place in Wales. Once I went to Ireland with a group of student friends and we stayed in a farmhouse. Nothing very adventurous but nice social trips.

At 21 I didn't really know what I wanted to do after university. At one point I was interested in making maps – it was an outdoor life which involved some travelling and I thought a maths degree might qualify me for it. I also thought about trying for the civil service or becoming a lawyer.

Bruce at 21, on the idea of going into the church:
'. . . if whatever I was doing I was doing very successfully, then that would be a better reason for going into the church really. Or at least, if I did go into the church it would mean I was giving up something for it. But I think the wrong reasons are if you're dissatisfied with what you're doing, you know, in a general sense of doing a job badly or . . . a failure in some sort of way.'

On politics:
'I am still Socialist but not as energetically as I was . . . I'm glad the Socialists are in power because the elusive thing called freedom is rearing its head and the Conservatives are pushing it forward . . . it really is exceptionally dangerous because the more you try and defend freedom – I mean you allow everybody to do exactly what they like within limits – then the less you have. I mean, there's no freedom in . . . living in a slum . . .'

On his mother's divorce:
'. . . as far as . . . my mother's divorce, I don't think that really has the effect that people imagine it to have. I mean, I always have got on well with my stepfather and with my half-sister. In that sense I've had a family life.'

On his father:
'. . . it's something I regret that I didn't get to know him better at all. We're both very bad writers. I'm probably worse than him and personally I regret not having established a regular correspondence because I think he's an interesting man, and he probably regrets it as well.'

On himself:

'I never want to feel too proud. It's dangerous for a start and it's so easy. And it doesn't work . . . because, all right, I can try and pretend to be humble, but that's being proud in just the same sort of way and I find it a very difficult thing to avoid pride.'

On religion:

'It all springs from loving God and Christ, I suppose. You try and do that as best as possible and let that lead your actions in life.'

On sex:

'I, as it were, burnt my fingers a little and I don't feel as though I'm missing anything now . . . I think there are two different sorts, casual sex and there's sex in love and marriage . . . Casual sex . . . I don't think it's quite as widespread as people believe because if both the people treat it as casual sex then I think it's all right. But if you're sort of looking for – I don't know, this may seem awfully silly – but if you're looking for casual sex and you don't want to treat it as such, then it doesn't seem to be worth the lies . . .'

Bruce at 35:

'I do regret not having worked harder at Oxford but it's something you did at the time so you accept it . . . I might well at some stage try and do a further degree in maths, or if not maths, perhaps a further degree in education or something else.'

Bruce graduating from Oxford University.

6 I think I possibly get a little serious and don't quite understand the modern . . . way of behaving, the modern manner. I think I'm a little old-fashioned. **9**

After Oxford I didn't exactly know what I wanted to do and I hadn't applied for any jobs so I ended up doing private tuition for a year – mainly maths O-level retakes. I was sharing a flat with two friends and it was a very pleasant year but I realised I was just marking time. So I went along to the

Appointments Board at Oxford and they said, 'Well, you've got maths and you can angle yourself this way.'

I must have applied for about half a dozen jobs and then an insurance firm in the City took me on as a trainee actuary. I ended up in the accounts department, still as a trainee. I can see why some people would be very happy doing such work but I really didn't find it very fulfilling. You just went into the office, did your work, came back and that was it.

I mean, I wasn't very clued-up when I went round to the Appointments Board. I didn't go along and say, 'I expect this, this and this,' and I got perfectly good advice as far as they were concerned. But working at it for nearly three years, I suppose I didn't get a lot out of it.

At the time I was lodging in Crystal Palace with an old family friend who was herself a teacher. And she said, 'Well, you can always become a maths teacher.' I hadn't realised it was a possibility but they were so short of maths teachers then that they would take anyone with a maths degree. It was so easy it was ridiculous. I just took a long lunch hour, walked along to Morpeth Comprehensive in Bethnal Green and had a look round. They phoned me the next day and said, 'Would you like the job?' And that was it.

Bruce at 28.

I look back on the whole episode with complete incredulity now. First of all I gave myself a week to prepare. I had planned to visit the school again, look at syllabi, lesson plans, etc. but the school was closed for Easter. On my first day I arrrived at about 7 a.m. feeling apprehensive. I could not remember where the maths department was. One teacher arrived after another. Eventually the Head of Maths appeared and said, 'Your first lesson is 2T now – then you are free. I will tell you the rest then.' The question, 'What on earth do I do with 2T?' died on my lips as he disappeared. On the second day a boy asked me what a quadrilateral was. I replied, 'Remember your Latin.' Wishing to make an impression in the staffroom – which I certainly did – I expressed a desire to see the Head of Classics as I wanted to know why a 13-year-old did not know his Latin. I stayed at this comprehensive for three years but, while having many happy memories, I was told that there had been a book opened as to how long I would last and that the longest option had been half-term.

When they made *28 Up* I'd moved to Daneford School, still in the East End, but a boys' school and at that stage about 50 per cent Bangladeshi. By coincidence it was also Tony Walker's old school. That first term at Morpeth had been a nightmare but after that I started to enjoy teaching a lot more.

At 28 I was living in a hard-to-let council flat near Daneford School. It was actually a very nice flat although I was thinking of trying to buy my own place. At that time I had a sort of girlfriend. It was a friendship that became something more serious, but only for a short time.

I'd joined the Labour Party a couple of years earlier and was a fairly active member. My stepfather had always been a Labour voter and maybe it was discussions with him that started me thinking that way. I was also going to the services at my local church quite regularly. In my spare time I used to play cricket in the summer and football in the winter. And I'd go and see my family during school holidays. Sophie and I still got on very well although I remember once pacing the streets when she was late coming home one night. But I gave up playing the older brother when she was about 18.

My father came back to England to retire when I was 24 or 25, and by the time I was 28 he'd settled in Yorkshire, where he was born. I used to go up there once a year or so to see him. We were always pleased to see each other, but I suppose we had drifted apart. He remarried and was very well looked after. Apparently he had a daughter from his first marriage, the one before he married my mother. I've been told that I met that sister when I was about eight but I have no recollection of it. I know where she lives now so I might get in touch at some stage.

Bruce at 28, on teaching:
'[The most enjoyable thing is] . . . just being a part of people's advancement and learning and watching them understand more and being more confident.'

On his own education:
'General education is better for society, I think. Public schools are divisive . . . My education was academically excellent and I was very grateful for it . . . [But] I think there is a class society and I think public schools may help its continuance.'

On politics:
'It seems to me that the leader of the country at the moment [Margaret Thatcher] should be one of the most unpopular people in the country. And yet she gets away with everything. She, as far as I can see, has done lots of damage and yet nobody can oppose her.'

'I just see the lack of opportunities for a lot of people. Obviously unemployment is a great feature in many . . . families' lives. And teaching children, sometimes you wonder what's going to happen to them.'

On immigration:
'. . . those who say too many are coming in and so on, I think really are uneducated about the whole question. They should see the positive benefits that they're having in this country . . . It's not the fault of immigrants that there is unemployment. It's part of a political party's responsibility to explain that . . .'

On religion:
'. . . if [people] dismiss it as just being something – oh well, we know about that, we got a little bit of that at school and it doesn't really mean very much – then it does sadden me because, you know, it's much, much more than that . . .'

'. . . the belief in goodness and in love as being two, well, great positive forces. And . . . just a simple belief like, a good act is never wasted.'

On himself:
'I think I would very much like to become involved in a family, my own family for a start. That's a need that I feel I ought to fulfil and would like to fulfil . . .'

'People probably say I'm a little innocent at times or naive. I used to get worried about this and think perhaps I ought not to be taken in or deceived – I'm not talking about love now, I'm just talking generally – but I feel that's a strength in a way, you know. I think if there are people willing to trust then, you know, we should be encouraged.'

Bruce at 35:
'When I first got the job at Morpeth Comprehensive they were a bit surprised at my choice at the office. And one chap very nicely said, "Well, look, you know, if you *are* making a mistake, don't feel too bad about it and get back in touch." So there was always an element of, well, if it doesn't work out . . . But I never really did think about going back to the insurance firm.'

The last programme, *28 Up*, introduced me with the following scene: a shot of me in the classroom amidst a crowd of Bangladeshi faces with a voice saying words to the effect, 'At the age of seven Bruce wanted to be a missionary . . .' There was then a brief pause before the voice continued, '. . . He is now teaching in the East End . . .'

This was, I suppose, an acceptable *ruse de guerre* for a documentary. Obviously my eventual profession can be interpreted as being a sort of failed missionary. I simply cannot point to any strong influence which led me to express that desire. But, having had such a desire at such an age, how can it be that it appears, albeit in a transmuted form, to have remained with me? Perhaps the adult is indeed like the child. They are the same person and that spark, which makes the individual, has a degree of constancy undimmed by later growing experiences.

Since *28 Up* I have been teaching for a further seven years at Daneford School which now has a great majority of Bangladeshis. That I am teaching a population which may have been served by missionaries in the past is a complete fluke, I insist. I am not a natural teacher in that I do not have instant control, but I have established myself, enjoy organising things for the boys, and have led classes to reasonable exam results. Over the past few years teaching has become very difficult. There have been so many changes – the GCSE being brought in, the ILEA breaking up, the new National Curriculum, local management of schools, teacher appraisal. It goes on and on, and sometimes you just feel that the changes should stop and we should get on top of what's already been done.

Bruce at 35.

Nevertheless I have a definite feeling of helping a community and particular families. I sense that I belong and have a place, and there is just as much in me receiving this sense of belonging as there is in me giving help in the form of an education and opportunities for the boys. I have found fulfilment here, and if I do leave I know that it will be a great wrench.

I think the way we teach now is actually a lot better for children than the way I was taught. I mean, I had an excellent traditional education but we do listen to pupils a bit more and try to respond to their particular requirements. In fact next term I'm going to Bangladesh on a three-month research trip, looking at how they teach maths over there. Then, even though some of our students can't speak much English we might still be able to teach them maths appropriate to their ability. I'm looking forward to the trip. I'll have to pay all my own expenses, but I think I'll be able to live quite cheaply out there.

Shortly after *28 Up* I bought a little flat in Hackney. It's near enough for me to cycle to work and I wanted somewhere in a nice open area, the sort of place where you could go out jogging or just get a feeling of space. The flat has one bedroom and it's quite comfortable. It's on the ground floor of a two-up, two-down terrace house with a little garden, and there's a park nearby.

I'm still a member of the Labour Party although I haven't been to a meeting for a long time. I'm not disillusioned – I'd just rather have the leisure time instead and my job keeps me fairly busy. I suppose if I do go to the odd evening meeting it's usually something to do with the church rather than the Labour Party. There has been a bit of a shift – I felt I couldn't do both.

I have girlfriends occasionally but things don't seem to work out somehow. I mean, sometimes I end the relationship and sometimes the other person does. It may be that I go about things the wrong way – possibly I'm still too old-fashioned about relationships. I'd probably live with someone before we got married, but I'd like to be married at some stage and I would like to have children. And, you know, I don't despair. I mean, something might happen tomorrow. I probably would like it to happen, on balance. But it doesn't always happen to everybody.

My father died about three years ago. He was 72. I used to phone my stepmother once a week or so and find out how he was. It was a bit unexpected when he died – I'd been planning to go up there at half-term – but I knew he hadn't been well. And you always feel a bit guilty. I probably hadn't seen him for a year or two before he died.

As each programme approaches I do examine my life closely and there are both satisfactions and regrets. I'm very happy teaching but I suppose a careers adviser would say, 'You ought to be a head of department by now . . .' In fact, I'm very comfortable here and perhaps I'm limiting my ambitions because I'm so comfortable. In some ways I'd like to have staff working for me because you can help them through their start in teaching, and that sort of human management has its own rewards.

I got into teaching almost accidentally. I think it must be very difficult to lead a planned life because you don't know what career opportunities or personal situations may arise. It takes a lot out of life if you say, 'By this time I should be doing this or that . . .'

I suppose I haven't quite got the job that was expected of me, and I think initially my parents were a bit disappointed but they're very happy now. As for the friends I made at Oxford – one's a civil servant, one's a journalist, one's training to be a lawyer, one's an academic – they're fascinated by the fact that I teach in an inner-city school. It's a life that a large proportion of people in this country possibly don't really come across, and they're fascinated by it.

We do live in a class-ridden society and I suppose the original documentary was a sort of polemic about class. I hope the class structure is dissolving – it was probably more marked in 1963, when the first programme was made, than it is now.

Taking part in the programmes has influenced my life in some ways (an example of the classic sociological phenomenon of the survey affecting the outcome). Apart from prompting me to examine my life periodically, there has been a friendship with Neil, being put up on my travels when in California, pupils running up the corridor making comments on my youthful ears or girlfriends in Africa, and comments made by strangers in letters which are almost always friendly and considerate.

Bruce at 35.

Bruce's mother:
'He said when he was a child that he wanted to be a missionary but there are all sorts of missionaries – religious missionaries, teaching missionaries . . . So perhaps he's fulfilling that early pledge . . .'

JACKIE

❛I would like to get married when I grow up. Well, I don't know what sort of boy but I think one that's not got a lot of money but he has got some money. ❟

I have four sisters. The eldest one was Janice – we always called her Janey – she was four years older than me. Then there was Lorraine, who I always called Ray. She was two years older than me. Then there was myself. My younger sister was Chris and she was two years younger than me, and the baby was Debbie. In fact Debbie was born just before we did the *Seven Up* programme, and I suppose that was the biggest thing in my life at the time. I can remember everyone being totally disappointed at first because she was another girl. I'm sure my father would have loved a son but us girls weren't really worried whether or not we had a brother. If Mum had had a little boy he wouldn't have stood much of a chance would he, with us four?

As children, Ray and I didn't get on at all. Everything sisters could do to one another we probably did. And my eldest sister, Janey, was so placid that it wouldn't have entered her head to have had the sort of arguments we had. So she'd be trying to act as peacemaker and invariably the youngest one would end up crying because Ray and I was going at it hammer and tongs. Basically it was just nit-picking at each other all the time, trying to get at one another. Mum used to get really fed up with all the arguing, although we used to do a lot of it when she wasn't about.

Home was cramped. We were in a three-bedroomed flat. It probably didn't feel that cramped at the time, but it must have been. There were three of us – myself and my two younger sisters – sharing a room. But it was all right, I mean, we managed, although I don't really know how. We were always being moaned at to put the toys away because there wasn't enough room. And I remember being cold in winter. Originally there was a coal fire. Then I think we got a gas fire, but we never had central heating, and the flat was right on the end of the block so the end bedroom used to get really cold. Mind you, we had blankets galore and we had each other to keep us warm. You'd wake up the next morning and find you were in bed with somebody else! In fact, we were always two and two – my two older sisters, myself and my younger sister, and then there was Debbie. Depending which of us wasn't really doing anything, they'd get Debbie.

We must have been a handful. Dad was great – he always helped – but Mum didn't actually go to work until my youngest sister went to school. Mum used to cook stew for us – I hated it and I still do. Most of the time we'd have meat and two veg, egg and chips, or something like that. Usually we had school lunches and then Mum gave us our dinner before Dad came in, because he was often home late. It was really only at holiday times that we'd all sit down and eat together, and obviously on Sundays. Sunday lunch used to be a real family meal with a big roast. Dad would get up and help Mum on Sunday mornings. Then he'd go to the pub and we'd go round to my nan's and wait for Mum and Dad to come home. And invariably we used to nick the meat and potatoes from my nan while we were at her house. I remember drinking the meat juice, as the meat was finishing cooking. I can still taste it!

At seven I was at Susan Lawrence School in Poplar, and I thoroughly enjoyed that school. I was one of the milk monitors who dished out the milk. It was all in the entrance to the school and we used to make everybody go out in the freezing cold playground while they drank it, and we didn't have to 'cos we were milk monitors! I can remember one of the teachers there – a Welsh teacher, and he always called me Bucket Head. I'd obviously done or said something that warranted it. It didn't upset me – in fact I'm sure we used to laugh about it.

I enjoyed playing netball and rounders a lot, and we used to do country dancing in the school hall. It wasn't that bad really, but we'd all try and get out of it – 'I've hurt me leg, Sir,' 'I've hurt me arm, Sir,' – anything to get out of it. Mr Enever used to say to the boys that if they wanted to be good footballers they should be good dancers 'cos then they'd have the balance. And the amount of boys that used to fall for it!

I was forever staying overnight at Sue's after school and at weekends. Sue

(*From left to right*)
Lorraine, Chrissy,
Janice and Jackie.

being an only child – I felt spoilt when I went there because there was only me and Sue, and there was one of everything. I know it sounds silly but you didn't have to share when you went to Sue's.

Jackie at 7, on fighting:
'It's really silly to fight 'cos if you fight and Miss comes into the classroom you only get told off.'

On her sisters:
'My mum . . . she's had seven years bad luck. That's why she's got five girls. And when the baby was about to be born we all wished it was a boy. Dad . . . visited her and he came home and said, "It's another girl, kids" and we said, "Aaahh . . ." '

On poor people:
'. . . 'cos if you don't help them they'd sort of die soon, wouldn't they? And every time we have Harvest Festival we send food to them . . . Susan and Janet went round giving it out with Mr Floyd . . .'

On coloured people:
'Well, they're nice. They're just the same as us really. But, one thing, it's only 'cos their skin's brown and we're white – sort of pinkish, we are.'

On her ambition when she grows up:
'I would buy myself a new house – one that's all nice and comfy.'

Jackie's father:
'She always talked a lot and wanted her own way a lot. If things had to be done she wanted to do them her way . . . She was a self-willed little madam . . .'

'She showed more promise than the others mentally . . . She did fairly well at school.'

Jackie at 35:
'My mum always said I was a late developer as far as talking was concerned, but I sure as hell made up for it! And that was me at seven. I didn't stop.'

'On the whole I look back . . . and I enjoyed my childhood – I really did . . . I suppose materially Mum and Dad would certainly have been happier with a lot more, but . . . somehow or other they always managed to get what we wanted. I don't know how they did it. Because at the end of the day they never really had two halfpennies to rub together.'

AT 14

❝ I would like to have a happy family. I mean, I know that it's not possible to be happy all the time but as much of the time as possible. ❞

At 14 I was at St Paul's Way Comprehensive. It was brand new when we went in, but it didn't take us long to wreck it! I was there with Sue, although by this time I'd moved to Hainault so I had to do the journey on my own.

As we got older we got very friendly with the teachers and that was a bonus. The teachers that I liked, I could usually get on with their subjects. So a lot of it did depend on how I reacted to the teachers. I actually got better results in English than I did in maths and yet maths was probably my strongest subject. I suppose at the time maths wasn't what you'd call a popular subject so I let it go, to a degree. And I do regret that.

I loved doing music and drama – we got out of lessons to do rehearsals! Basically I was pretty lazy. But Sue and I did a lot of drama outside school as well. If the truth be known, Sue was a lot better at it than I was but we used to boost one another. We actually did a couple of pantomimes for kids in the local theatre and that was great. We were 14 or 15 but we thought we were totally grown up.

I was never particularly into pop music. My older sisters were always putting the radio on or playing records so I suppose I was brought up with sixties music, but I only heard it 'cos of them or my aunt. I think I'd like to have been into fashion but I never really had the money to be. And, to be honest, I was totally the wrong shape for all the fashions. I hated the fact that I was overweight, but I wasn't really prepared to do anything about it. I hated mini-skirts – I wore them but I hated them because of my fat legs. In the end I wore clothes that I thought hid everything, and in fact they made it worse.

Jackie at 14.

As for boys, there were obviously people you had a crush on but really I wasn't that interested. It was all good fun and maybe something to talk to your friends about, but that was it.

For holidays, Dad often used to take us to holiday camps. We went to the Isle of Wight one year and it absolutely poured down from the minute we got there to the minute we left. We had this old army tent. There were all these brand new ones around us, but we were as dry as dry can be and all the brand new ones went floating down the field! We had some good holidays and there was always a crowd of us because my mum and dad always used to go away with family – whether it be mother-in-law, sister-in-law, cousins or whatever. It was good fun and there was always someone of your own age. At about 14 I went to Malta with a friend from school and her parents. I loved the country and I loved flying in the aeroplane. The thought of it terrified me but, when it came to it, it was really good.

I used to see Lynn after school up until I was about 11, but once I went on to St Paul's Way I hardly ever saw her.

Jackie at 14, on strikes:

'They're going to strike for it [the money], right? They're going to get more money, the school meals are going up, so that means they're going to strike again, they want more money. And they're just going to keep going and going and going.'

On rich people:

'Some people are just born into rich families and they are lucky.'

On Britain in the future:

'. . . there's quite a few people I know who have got homes that are miles too small and I think I would like to see that all changed . . .'

On religion:

'I don't really know if I do [believe in God] or not . . . That's the sort of thing I'd like to sit and think about or talk to someone about.'

On her ambition:

'Just to live comfortable . . . just so long as you've got all you need.'

Jackie's father:

'She'd go out and invariably she was either 20 minutes or half an hour later than she said . . . Their mother used to go mad at them and then I was only dragged in if Mother couldn't cope. Fortunately they all respected me and if I was on the war path they knew they had to look out.'

Jackie at 35:

'Sometimes I wish I'd done things slightly different. Certainly I wish I'd paid more attention to what some of the teachers were saying at the time . . . It would have been a lot easier . . . I suppose I look on 14 as being an embarrassing time – I was very conscious of everything. Though, judging by the way I'm dressed in the photo at 14, you wouldn't have known it! But the embarrassment was probably what made me as loud and brash as I was. At the end of the day if I didn't let anyone in close enough then they couldn't get to me. Really, I was very, very unsure of myself.'

AT 21

'If you think that being married as far as we're concerned is a case of going to work, coming home and cooking tea for hubby, going to bed, getting up, going to work, you're totally mistaken. ,

I met Mick at a local pub where a mutual friend was celebrating his birthday. When we left, Mick said that he was going to walk me home, which was totally out of his way. To be honest, I wasn't that bothered whether he did or not. And that seems to sum up our life together – things just seemed to happen rather than us making them happen. Neither of us would say that it was love at first sight but we had a good life together, I think.

I got married at 19 and the cake collapsed at the wedding reception – it must have been an omen! In fact, I kept one layer of that wedding cake until three years ago because, traditionally, you're supposed to keep it for your first child's christening. But I'd decided then that I was never having children so I threw it out.

Having had to pay for my sisters' weddings, my father did try to persuade us to elope but we didn't take any notice, and it proved a very expensive time for my parents. The only thing I actually bought was my wedding dress.

Mick and I bought a three-bedroomed house in East Tilbury – I loved that house but I didn't particularly like the area. The house was two years old when we bought it so the people before us had done the hard work. It had a garden, front and back, not very big but big enough for us. Mick just mowed the lawn occasionally and pruned the roses.

I remember once we'd bought a new three-piece suite and Mick was in the garden demolishing the old one so we could dump it. He was hitting this old three-piece with a hammer and I was standing in the kitchen getting the dinner ready, when suddenly the hammer came flying through the window and swished past my ear. There was glass everywhere – the hammer had just flown out of his hand. And he turned round, looked at me and started laughing! We had to fill the window in with perspex – I think it was still there when we sold the house.

We were absolutely broke, like most newly-weds I suppose. When I think about it now, we should never have had the wedding – we should have used the money towards the house. When they were filming *21 Up*, Mike wanted me to give Sue a tour of the house and we had to pretend it was all spontaneous when we'd already done it about six times.

I left school with CSEs in English and maths, but I remember flunking French completely. I didn't do that bad but by today's standards it wasn't that good. Anyway I got a job with a bank. They wanted you to have done the course and sat your exams at least, but it didn't really matter at that time how well you'd done. Maybe I'm wrong, but you give me someone with common sense over exam results any day of the week. We had one girl come in with O-levels and A-levels as long as your arm but she didn't have an ounce of common sense. She ended up re-addressing mail. At the end of the day, if you can't do the job no qualification's going to make any difference.

When I was working at the bank you moved about and learnt about all different areas – foreign currency and foreign exchange, dealing with the client mailing system, that type of thing. You'd spend a certain length of time here and a certain length of time there, and I liked the variety.

By the time I was 21 my younger sister, Chris, was just getting married, so my parents only had Debbie left at home. My in-laws lived not far from them, so we was always backwards and forwards.

Mick and I often used to go out for Indian meals, but I suppose our social life centred around the local pub. We had plenty of friends in the area – Geoff, our next-door neighbour, was brilliant – but I've only kept in touch with one or two. Although we'd already been engaged for eight months and married a couple of years, we were still getting to know one another. I'd have preferred it if we'd lived together for a while before we got married but we never even talked about it. Strange really, because my older sister lived with her boyfriend.

I was never very ambitious in my career – I always found it a bit difficult trying to handle working and the home, although Mick was pretty good in the house. As long as I was happy where I was working then that suited me.

Jackie at 21, on her wedding day:
'It was a funny day actually. Two of my friends and I were up till around five o'clock. And I spent all day preparing – well, all morning, I should say, and then sitting around for about three hours just waiting for something to happen, and when it did happen I don't really remember it happening. It was just complete confusion really . . .'

'I can't forget the cake. It was horrific . . . what happened to the wedding cake. It was sitting between Mick and myself and suddenly the columns gave way and fell into one.'

On her career:
'At the moment my career is about the furthest thing from my mind. I don't really know what I'm aiming for except getting the house together. That can take years . . .'

On decorating the house:
'Friends had some paint handy so Dad and Mick just sort of used the roller and in one day it was done. Two coats, wallop, that was it.'

Jackie at 21.

On money:
'When you reach the 18th day of the month and my mortgage is due on the 20th and there's nowhere near enough money in there, I get depressed about it obviously. You suddenly think, oh my God, what's going to happen? . . . But it gets there. Don't ask me how, but you get it.'

Jackie at 35:

'I don't feel my lack of qualifications has really held me back because I went into the bank straight from school, then I went temping for a while. One of the companies took me on and they knew I could do the job, so I suppose I've been lucky. If I'd wanted to be a teacher or go on further then, yes, it would have been a problem.'

' I don't think, to be honest, we consciously think about class until this programme comes up once every seven years. **,**

When I was 28, Mick had been out of work for a while. That was very tough – tougher for me than it was for him in certain respects. In the end he just accepted the fact that he couldn't get work. He's the type of person who can turn his hand to anything, so I suppose I felt he wasn't trying hard enough.

Things got a bit better when he became self-employed, and just after they made *28 Up* we sold the house, stayed with one of my aunts for six months and then started running a pub in Cambridgeshire. Myself, my husband and my mum and dad – all four of us went into it together, and I loved every minute of it. I loved the contact with people. It's long hours and it can be hard work but, with the right partner, it can be really good.

Moving from London to Cambridgeshire was frightening at first. It was like moving to The Land Time Forgot. Nobody knows what quick is out there. They've only got two paces – stop and dead stop! But once I got used to it I absolutely adored it. The locals were used to Londoners – quite a few of the pubs round there are run by ex-Londoners.

At that point we definitely didn't want children. In fact, it would have been a good time to have done so, because, with the four of us there, it would have given me time to have brought up the child.

Jackie at 28, on marriage:

'I'm not sure I would recommend it [marrying young] . . . I would say on average 19 is probably too young.'

On her decision not to have children:

'Basically I'd say . . . I'm far too selfish. I enjoy doing what I want when I want . . . and certainly at the moment I can't see any way around that. That's not to say that that's a forever decision. Some people can make it work – I just don't think I could.'

'I do feel, to a degree that, yes, I'm missing out, but I also think that I get far more pleasure – or I'm gaining far more experience – by not having that tie.'

On education:

'Most parents would want every advantage that they can get for their child. Now, whether you class going to grammar school as an advantage is dependent on your entire outlook. If you don't class it as an advantage then you're not going to push that.'

On herself:

'I don't think I have [changed] really . . . the basics are there [at seven] . . .'

On class:

'If you've got a comfortable background then perhaps it can make life easy, but I think you've also seen within this programme that it doesn't always work that way.'

Jackie's father:

'My idea was to run the pub for a few years and then retire and leave it to them . . . In the end we ran it together for about two years and we didn't get in each other's way because we were able to take a few days off here and there alternatively . . . I don't think it could have been a long-term thing because we've both got the same nature . . . She takes after me more than the others. We've got the same forceful personality, to put it mildly.'

Jackie at 28.

'What happened with her marriage happens with thousands . . . At the time I couldn't really see any problems . . .'

Jackie at 35:

'At 28, life was really starting to change because of the pub . . . and it was the start of all the changes that have happened since. I obviously didn't know that at the time but it was the start of another life really.'

I suppose the most horrendous thing that's happened in the last few years was Mum dying. It all happened so fast. One minute we were in the pub and everything was going great guns. Then Mick and I split up. Mum was already ill at that point, although we didn't realise how bad it was. She had cancer, and suddenly Dad was having to spend more time with her.

We couldn't keep the pub going. Dad just wasn't interested, which was understandable. So we moved out of the pub and I lived in a bungalow in Cambridgeshire for a while and Mum and Dad went back to London. As Mum got worse, I began to spend more and more time in London and eventually I moved in with my sister Ray. And then Mum died. She was only 53, we'd all left home and my parents' life together was just beginning again. It just seems so unfair, so totally unfair. She spent all her life looking after us and making sure we were all right. And when it came to the time when she and Dad should have been able to enjoy themselves – she died. So, no one will ever give me 'Life's fair'.

Dad didn't cope at all at first. I remember him talking to people in the pub about it – Mum was upstairs because she wasn't well enough to come down – and he'd say if anything ever happened to her that would be it, his life would be over. And I remember saying to him, 'That's a selfish attitude. That's the time we would need you.' And I didn't really understand it at the time. It was only afterwards that I realised just how bad it must have been for him. I mean, I know how bad I felt, so God knows what he must have felt. They'd been a couple for so long – they'd known each other since he was 16 or 17 – and suddenly she wasn't there. Silly things, like birthday reminders, she wasn't there to tell him any more.

I lived with him for a while after Mum died but in the end we both knew that I couldn't stay there. I moved out into a flat of my own, literally 200 yards down the road. At least, to a degree, we were independent. And then about 18 months after Mum died he said he was going to take a friend out for a drink. I was relieved because by this time I was wondering whether he could live without me and he was wondering whether I had any life other than him. He was so depressed – anybody that knew him knew he wasn't the same man. Then he met Eryl and she's a lovely lady. They get on really well and he's got something in his life that he needed desperately. My mother would be happy for him – I don't think she'd expect Dad to live on his own. I mean, he could live to be 100! Now I have to make an appointment to see him, and I'm so glad.

Mick and I were together just short of ten years. We broke up when I was about 29. The whys and wherefores I don't think are that important. What is important is that we both managed to deal with it and we're probably better friends now than we've ever been. He's in a relationship and he's got a young son who's absolutely gorgeous.

I had a few years when I was on my own but now I'm set up in my own life. Although Mick and I are still good friends it's a phase of my life that is totally over. And, whilst I look back on it and I enjoyed the time, nothing really stands out. I feel as though my life started again when we split up.

Mick and I decided long ago that we didn't want children, yet now we've both got them. I couldn't believe it when I got pregnant. I went through the usual what shall I do's and don'ts, and decided that I desperately wanted to keep the child. When he was born I took one look at him and he was so like my dad I had to call him Charlie. At the time I was living with Ray and her husband, Keith. My brother-in-law's always been very good to me, so I called my son Charles Keith. Charlie has transformed my life completely. I'd never have believed it possible. He can be a little so and so, like most kids, but I adore everything about him. He's nearly 17 months old now and he gets more interesting as time goes on.

Jackie at 35.

The thought of motherhood used to terrify me, but I really enjoy it. I stopped working in the February and I had Charlie in May. I didn't know what I wanted to do, so I didn't take maternity leave, I just left the company I was with. I'd always said I'd go back to work after a few months. In fact it was nearly a year before I went back. But I knew I wanted to go back, for me more than anything. I'd have survived on the money but I knew that being at home all day I would probably have ended up getting tense with Charlie, and it certainly wouldn't have occupied me enough.

I've only been back at work about five months so, at the moment, I'm still finding my feet. I'm working to try and make life a little better for Charlie and myself. Luckily, I've got a child-minder who's a very good friend and she adores Charlie. It's worked out really well.

And recently I've met someone who's changed my life again. I just can't believe how much has happened in the last few years. My life has turned around totally. From being single with no worries at all, I'm suddenly a mother and I'm in a relationship that hopefully is going to work out really well. If someone had told me five or six years ago what my life was going to be like when I reached 35 I'd never have believed them. I still don't believe it.

Have I changed much? I suppose I've learnt occasionally to keep my mouth shut, but not very often. I've always got something to say about something. I think that really sums me up right through my life – not just at seven and 14 but even now. I'm still very unsure of myself but a lot of people who think they know me wouldn't acknowledge that.

Where would I like to be in seven years' time? I'd like to think that my life would be settled – whether that means in another relationship or on my own with Charlie, I don't know. Overall these last seven years have proved to me that I'll never ever be settled. My life will probably still be changing when I'm 65. And I don't really care. The more it changes, to a degree, the better. As long as I've still got that stable background of my family there, then I'll never ever be on my own. And now I've got Charlie too.

Jackie's father:
'I don't think Jackie's ever realised her full potential but then maybe the opportunities haven't come along . . . The job she does she's good at. Maybe if she'd been able to stick at it . . . but the marriage, the baby, the death of her mother, sort of broke it all up . . .'

'When my wife died Jackie stayed with me to keep me company. I suppose it's brought us closer although I try not to admit it because it looks as if I'm favouring one of my daughters above the others . . . I have the same attitude with all of them – they know I'm there if they need me.'

Charlie and Jackie.

LYNN

'I'm going to work in Woolworths. ' **AT 7**

One of my strongest memories is from long before I was seven. For instance I vividly remember going to nursery, even though it's so long ago. We used to have to take cod liver oil. They'd give it to you on a spoon and when the children wouldn't take it they used to fling it on the fire. It was a big open fire and I remember the way it flared up when they threw the oil on it. I hid under the bed and they had to send for my Mum to find me because I wouldn't come out. I didn't eat or drink for a week, so I never went back.

Another memory is of our local priest when I was little. He used to walk round the area in this great big cloak and there would always be four or five kids underneath it. Everyone loved him and they actually named the local park after him.

Later on I remember the Church secretary bringing the Lent boxes round to our house for us to put money in, and then throughout Lent she'd come round, shake the box and tell you there wasn't enough in it. She was a great character trotting up and down the street with her boxes.

When I was seven we were living in a second floor flat in Poplar in the East End. The flat had two bedrooms and I shared a room with my sister Pat who was eight years older. We got on well although there was a bit of an age gap. Dad was working as a coalman and I remember him coming home covered in black dust. Mum wasn't working at the time.

I went to Susan Lawrence School in Poplar and I was in the same class as Jackie and Susan. I enjoyed going there – I remember playing a lot of netball and rounders. Most of the teachers were very friendly. One special teacher commanded a lot of respect. He was fantastic as a teacher and as a person but if you saw him coming and shouting your name you knew you were in trouble. We set up a warning system and the shout of 'Bert alert' would send everyone running. There was a fantastic music teacher and we did operas. We did productions of *Amahl and the Night Visitors* and *The Mikado*. I got a part in the chorus because I couldn't sing in front of an audience on my own – I would lose my voice. I was also in the choir and later on played the recorder.

Jackie lived just over the road, so she often used to come round after school. She'd bring her younger sister with her. Susan lived further away and Jackie and I weren't allowed to walk that far on our own. When Jackie came over, we'd play dressing-up games or use orange boxes as pretend dolls' houses. And I can remember many a time my mum coming in and telling us not to jump on the beds. 'Don't you jump on that bed any more or I'll send you home!'

I ran away once. Well, I went across the main road on my own when I wasn't supposed to. I wanted to go to the park and it was on the other side of the road. I got into a lot of trouble for that. We used to play Knockdown Ginger – knocking on people's doors and running away. We were never caught for that but I remember once being accused of something I hadn't done. One of our neighbours said I'd thrown a stone which broke her window. I'd been on a Brownies' outing so there was no way it could have been me, but she was insistent that it was. In the end Mum got Brown Owl and took her down to the neighbour's house to prove my innocence.

Mum and Dad took Pat and me on holiday to the Lake District, where it usually rained. And at weekends we'd go on family outings to the seaside, to Brighton, Clacton or Southend. When I was on my own, I was always reading. I grew up on Enid Blyton's school stories – St Clare's – I just couldn't get enough of those.

Lynn at seven.

Lynn at 7, on money:
'If I had lots of money I'd help the poor.'

On children:
'I'd have two girls and two boys.'

Lynn's father:
'At seven she was stubborn and independent.'

Lynn at 35:
'Let me clarify why I did actually say I wanted to work in Woolworths . . .
Literally because my sister had just started work part-time in Woolworths . . .
It was her first job.'

'I think I was a lot shyer at seven. I didn't tend to stand up for myself.'

AT 14

6 Grammar school is fantastic . . . This is my first choice . . . even though some of my friends are going to the other school. 9

We were still living in the flat in Poplar. Dad was working for London Transport as a bus inspector and Mum was a kitchen assistant in a local school in the daytime. She also had a cleaning job for an hour each evening. Pat had just completed her BSc degree course at London University, and had started work as a dietary adviser.

Dad and my sister had both been to another local grammar school. I didn't want to go to the same one because it would have been, 'Oh your sister could do that.' I was given the choice – Mum and Dad never forced me, they advised me – and I decided to go to George Green Grammar School.

At 14 I was having a whale of a time. I was always good at maths – till it came to the exams. When we started the O-Level course we were split into arts or sciences, and you couldn't mix the two. I suppose I was a good all-rounder. I could have gone either way but I chose the arts.

George Green's was a small, friendly school, though it was a bit old fashioned; boys and girls were separated at break times. I don't think I had a special boyfriend then. I mean, I had friends who were boys but in those days you didn't start going out with boys at 14. We went around as a group.

I remember being in the music society and again, we were very lucky with our music teacher. There was an opera company who used to rehearse at the Troxie in Stepney and Mum used to get free tickets and take me to see them. We'd go to Sadler's Wells with the school sometimes. We all played the

Lynn at 14.

recorder and we were given the opportunity to have piano lessons at school.

I was too young to go to pop concerts although a group of us did go up to the West End to see 'The Monkees' at the hotel where they were staying. We stood outside with thousands of others screaming and shouting till they came out. The first record I bought was 'Bridge Over Troubled Water' by Simon and Garfunkel.

As for clothes, minis were still in but maxis were starting to come in too. I had a brown tweed maxi coat but I've never really been one to follow the fashions. I've always been me, and worn what I felt comfortable in. I used to wear cords with 'Ban the Bomb' signs all over them and names of all my favourite groups – Led Zeppelin, Beatles, Bowie, etc. I was into bells and chains and had an Afghan coat. Mum used to laugh and say to Dad, 'You're not going out with her wearing that, are you.' He would say 'I don't care what she looks like,' and out we'd go. Mum was the same though because she didn't mind what I looked like, as long as I was healthy and OK they didn't mind.

In my spare time, I liked playing badminton, going ice-skating when I could afford it, and swimming. I still loved reading – mainly historical novels and crime stories. When I read the newspaper it was usually the *Daily Mirror* or the *People*.

At 14 I was also helping to run a cub scout group once a week for seven-year-olds. And I was going to a church 'Open house' for teenagers set up by the local priest. He was very young and trendy – we used to call him 'Hippy Dave'. The house was always open to anyone who wanted to go – it was very, very casual and relaxed. You could stay for several hours or just have a coffee and leave. And that was the start of it. Everyone called him Dave and the whole atmosphere in the parish became more relaxed.

Some of my friends were starting to smoke dope but I wasn't interested. They didn't try to persuade me because by then they knew that if I said no I meant no. Even though I started smoking not long after, I never smoked a joint. I just didn't want to know. My friends never really got into trouble with drugs. They just tried it and then went on to something else. They're all living very respectable lives now.

I very rarely saw Jackie and Susan during our time at secondary school. They had their friends from their school and we had our groups and the two didn't really mix. I saw them occasionally but I'd probably see Sue's mum and dad more than I saw Sue.

Lynn at 14, on money:
'Money can't buy happiness . . .'

On rich people:
'They're just the same as us, really . . . Somewhere in the family there must
be someone who must have worked for it.'

On politics:
'I'm not keen on the Tories. I'm not keen on Edward Heath. Take the last
mini Budget, for instance. They said they were going to put the tax down and
what do they do? They put it down sixpence and put everything else up!'

On strikes:
'If their wage is low and no one's going to raise it, why should they work?'

On her parents:
'They might say their opinion on certain things but mainly the choice
is left up to me.'

'If you've got a good background you're not likely to go wrong.'

Lynn at 15,
in her favourite hat.

On religion:
'Well someone must plan your life out for you and . . . well, your parents
can't tell you you're going to go out in the street and be knocked down, but
there must be someone that knows that . . . Maybe it's God. I don't know.'

On her future career:
'If I do get any A-Levels then I'll go on to teaching.'

Lynn's father:
'By 14 she'd added determination to stubbornness and independence and she
was determined to go her own way. There were one or two things . . . but she
soon sorted them out. I had every confidence in Lynn.'

Lynn at 35:
'By 14 I was standing on my own two feet. I suppose I was more grown-up in
general, but it was also the atmosphere in the school. It was a very small
school – you knew everybody.'

AT 21

‘ We had a teacher at school. His favourite ploy was, "All you girls want to do is go out, get married, have babies and push a pram down the street with a fag hanging out the side of your mouth." **,**

I started going out with Russ in my last year at George Green. He's got a different version of what happened than I have – haven't we all. After we had left school and were both working he wanted me to move in with him but I said, 'Not before we're married.' So we were engaged for a year. We had a very, very white wedding – everything was white. I was in white, my bridesmaid was in white and Russ wore a white suit with a midnight blue shirt, a big white kipper tie and a midnight blue carnation. Very stylish – except that he still had shoulder-length hair. He offered to get it cut but I was scared I wouldn't like it. He eventually had it cut about six months afterwards.

Our church in Poplar had closed down the summer before we got married so we had the wedding in another local church. Hippy Dave was originally going to marry us but by that time he'd left the parish. The reception was in the old church hall.

When I was 21 we were living in a terrace house – we managed to put down a £500 deposit and get a mortgage. We shared the money side of things although we each had our own bank accounts. At that stage we weren't planning to have any children for a good few years.

Russ and I were both working for Tower Hamlets Library Service, at one point doing more or less the same job. Then I got promoted and moved to a different department from Russ. When they made *21 Up* I was running a mobile library, visiting about eight schools a fortnight. Russ was working as a library assistant at Whitechapel Library.

There weren't any other young couples living in the street where we lived but we still saw our old schoolfriends. We used to go out on the odd binge after payday, to a pub or out for a meal. Russ will eat anything as long as it's edible. We would quite often visit friends' homes and as none of us had children we could come and go as we pleased. Often we'd spend the night on someone's floor. I used to shop in bulk once a month. We had a freezer and only needed to buy bread and milk during the week.

Lynn at 21.

In the evenings I'd often read reviews and children's books for work, or we'd watch telly or listen to the stereo. For holidays we'd go to the Norfolk Broads or Cornwall on Russ's motorbike. He didn't drive a car then, but I had a Vauxhall which I'd saved up for myself. I applied for my driving test on my seventeenth birthday – Dad taught me to drive, and I passed first time.

Lynn at 21, on marriage:
'I've been married a year and a couple of months. And I do think, "Christ what have I done?" And I'm being honest about it, and Russ thinks the same.'

On her job:
'Teaching children the beauty of books and watching their faces as books unfold to them is just fantastic.'

'I love working with children. You might remember on the last one I wanted to teach but I didn't get to that and seeing as it is today I'm glad I didn't . . . I think it takes a lot more patience than I've actually got – I'm much more at home here.'

Lynn and Russ.

On equal opportunities:
'I've had the opportunities in life that I've wanted.'

Lynn's father:
'They had a fine time at the reception – I was busy serving at the bar. Lynn looked marvellous.'

Lynn at 35:
'Isn't it strange at 21 there was a surplus of teachers and you couldn't get a job. Today they are screaming out for teachers. I'm still glad that I chose librarianship. I seem to be clarifying everything at 35. But my quote on marriage at 21 was taken quite out of context from the conversation. Who doesn't wonder why they have got married on occasions. It can't be that bad, we've been married for 16 years now, and still don't want to change each other.'

AT 28

‛ I've got no seething ambition to go out and conquer the world. ,

When they made *28 Up* we had two daughters, Emma, who was three, and Sarah who had just been born. I took maternity leave from my job in the library and Russ was working shifts as a postman. He used to help with the housework and looking after Emma. When I went back to work my Mum looked after Sarah during the day and took Emma to nursery and collected her. It was a long day and I sometimes didn't get in till 6.30.

Before Sarah was born we had moved to a bigger house, and this suited us even better. We had brilliant neighbours who would all help out when needed. Russ's main interest then was motorbikes. He used to buy lots of motorbike magazines and had an 1100cc bike which he used to ride to work. We often took the bike on holiday – before the children were born – on camping trips in Scotland.

Lynn and Sarah,
just after Sarah's birth.

Lynn at 28, on her job:
'To work with children of this age you've got to love them, and I love children.'

On marriage:
'It is a partnership, marriage . . . We married young but because we wanted to go out and have fun together and grow together.'

On her decision to go to grammar school:
'I don't think anybody influenced me. It was a conscious decision. Obviously it was discussed at home but it was always in me to go.'

On herself, Jackie and Sue:
'We're the same people as we were then [at seven] . . . I don't think one is set by that age. You progress but the overall character is there ... the basics are there. [We haven't changed much because] we've all had a stable background with stable relationships all the way through.'

Lynn's father:
'Lynn and Russ are well-suited. They were friends at school and . . . they're both hard workers.'

Lynn at 28.

Lynn at 35:

'Well things haven't changed much in the last seven years, just carry on reading.'

AT 35

Out of a hat!!!! That's how I first became involved in *Seven Up*. After our school had been contacted and asked to provide children to appear in a *World in Action* film. The head teacher put all the names of the class into a hat and pulled out several. Mine was originally a reserve name as they thought I would be too shy, but after contacting parents to get their agreement one girl dropped out and I replaced her.

We had great fun whilst filming *Seven Up*, with microphones on sugar bowls which were set on lunch tables. Of course they were not normally there – nor were the sugar bowls. Whilst being filmed watching TV we had to pretend and make all the noises as the TV was not actually on – in those days you didn't get AM TV. Queuing for Saturday morning pictures and being whisked away without getting in to see the film.

There had been five of us together for *Seven Up* but at 14 the two boys Leslie and Geoff were not filmed, just leaving us three girls, Jackie, Sue and myself. I didn't really enjoy filming *Seven Plus Seven* very much, as to me it was a 'set-up' with me being the one set up. As I was at grammar school – George Green – Mike seemed to make a big thing of trying to provoke arguments between the other two and myself. Of course a lot of it is not seen in the film but some of the chat got quite heated and I'm seen very vehemently saying, 'Grammar schools are great.'

At 21 I was already married to Russ. I agreed to be filmed at work – that was a revelation in itself. They wanted to film me at a school, so I contacted the head of St Matthias – unfortunately now closed – and asked if they would co-operate, and with the Chair of Governors – Father Bourne's – permission things went fine. But as I was filmed in the course of my work it had to be vetted by Tower Hamlets before they would clear its use – just in case I said anything detrimental. Fortunately I didn't and the Chief Librarian at the time gave it the OK.

Everyone was brought together at 21 and we had great fun chatting to the others and finding out what had been happening to them and seeing the

Lynn at 35.

changes that had occurred. Because of Granada I felt and still feel as if we are all friends and that for better or worse our lives are linked forever.

After *21* went on the air and over the following years I began to notice that student teachers who were working in some of the schools I visit, gaining teaching practice, were giving me funny looks. They were being shown the films as part of their training and after the first few times I just used to say, 'Yes it is me, which ones have you seen so far?' Depending on how many programmes they had seen I would give them a run down on the next and suggest comments they could make on them, telling them to say that they came 'Straight from the horse's mouth'. To this day I don't know if any of them did, but I'd like to think so.

By the time *28* came along I had two children, two beautiful girls: Emma, then three, and Sarah just born. When discussions were taking place about filming *28 Up* I was pregnant with Sarah and Mike tried his hardest to persuade me to be filmed giving birth. Sorry everyone but it was a very private time for us and no way was I going to agree to the whole world being present.

We all got together again shortly after the film won the BAFTA award for best documentary and we were all awarded our own little *28 Up* statue. It was the first time after the filming of *28 Up* that Granada said that they would be back to do another one. All the other times it had been a surprise phone call 'This is Granada television here, it's about . . .'

So that brings us to 35. I'm still married to Russ, the girls are ten and seven and yes I'm still doing the same job – really boring I hear you say, what on earth do they want to film her again for? I wonder too. But for me things have changed very little. It's the personal things which mean a lot and affect our lives so much which matter. At 33 I lost my Mum – this was a tremendous blow to me as not only was she the best mother in the world to me, she was also my best friend – but although not with us in body she is still with us in spirit and always will be. Coincidentally Tony's Mum and mine died in the same week.

When my girls were small I went back to work – I'm not the type to be at home all day. I was able to do this because of the support of my Mum. She had the girls for me. I'm really lucky, because after she died one of the first things my Dad said to me was, 'That's my job now,' and despite some health problems over the last two years he has coped with this tremendously. We love him very much. We have always been very close and are always on hand whenever needed. Russ's parents moved to Norfolk three years ago when my father-in-law lost his job in the Wapping print dispute, but again a phone call will bring them running.

Lynn, Russ, Emma (*right*) and Sarah.

Yes I'm still doing the same job. I hope that I do it well. Having been born and bred in Poplar I feel that I am giving back some of what Poplar gave and still gives to me by taking a service to children who for many reasons cannot actually visit a library. Having done the job for so long and expanded it to capacity with present staffing levels, one would think that it is time to move on. But every visit is a challenge, every new child is different, new teachers bring different ideas and new relationships are made all the time. I even learnt some Bengali so that I could speak to the children who cannot speak English. This is hilarious because sometimes they will rabbit away in Bengali and I will pick up some of what they are saying, and then they assume I can speak fluently, and I have to quickly say that I can only speak a little bit.

I am on the Governing bodies of two schools. On one I am appointed by Tower Hamlets as their representative – at the moment I am actually Chairperson. On the other I am Foundation parent governor, which means that I am elected by the other Foundation governors and this is the school where my girls are – hence the parent governor connection. This obviously takes up quite a bit of what little spare time we have. But it's all a matter of balance and even though there are times when there do not seem to be enough hours in the day, what with all the extra activities – netball, football, swimming etc – that the girls want to take part in, somehow it all fits together and still leaves us with enough time to go and see family and friends who are spread out all over the country and to do things together as a family which to me is the most important thing.

Lynn at work in the mobile library.

Lynn's father:

'I think things have worked out exceptionally well for Lynn. She's in demand at the library now. Everything's going on computer and she mastered it quickly and everyone asked her what to do. She copes with the pressures marvellously. It's even worse now, with the governorship. She sometimes doesn't get home till half past eight . . . She makes sure the girls do what they're told. She's strict enough but she can bend when necessary. If she and Russ want to go out for an evening they can always leave the girls with me.'

'Our relationship was there in the background all the time but since my wife died it's come out a bit more.'

'She's as mad as her father – but I wouldn't change her. And the girls are the same now. They know their own mind – they both take after Lynn.'

SUE

‘ Well, sometimes we go out and play nicely with the boys and sometimes we go out and argue with the boys. ’

When I was seven we lived in a house in Poplar. Nan lived with us – she had a room upstairs. And there was a yard. It had a little garden but we called it the yard and my dad was very proud of it. I remember my bedroom was downstairs and everybody else's was upstairs, and I was backing on to the yard. I was really frightened of that yard – maybe because the toilet was out there. (We didn't have an indoor bathroom – we used to have to get a tub in.) And up to this day I still have to have something round my neck when I'm asleep because I had this thing about vampires. I don't know where I got it from – I must have seen a film or something – but it plagued me when I was young, it really did.

During the day it was fine, it was a nice place to live. The house was opposite a bridge and it was in a quiet street. We used to play tennis and kick a ball against the wall of the bridge. We'd play elastics (French skipping) – I remember doing that in the back garden.

My dad was working as a cabinet maker, making furniture, and Mum had part-time jobs but she was always there when I came home after school. At the time I don't remember being that bothered about not having any brothers or sisters. My teacher told my mum how well-adjusted I was for an only child – probably because I wasn't throwing tantrums or demanding things. I used to get a lot of ribbing from other children about being a spoilt only child and I remember being jealous of Jackie with all her sisters. But the only way it really affected me was that it made me decide I'd never do it to my own

Sue at seven.

child. If I had one of my own I'd want to give them a brother or sister – that was really important to me.

We used to spend all our Christmas and school holidays at my mum's sister's house in Watford. She had two little girls called Jackie and Kim – one older and one younger than me – and it was like having two sisters. We always used to have loads of family parties – the family were very close.

At school, Susan Lawrence Primary, I got on well with the teachers and I wasn't a lot of trouble for anybody, except for one incident, which I still remember very clearly. Jackie and I used to have piano lessons in school. I don't know what made me do it – we may have been arguing about whose turn it was to play – but I remember dropping the piano lid down on Jackie's fingers. It's stayed on my mind as it's so unlike me. I haven't much of a temper.

My other memories of school are mainly of dressing up as fairies and flitting about in costumes at festivals and things. I can remember being in the choir because I've always loved to sing. The school was very sports-orientated and I hated sports at the time. I was terrified of being involved in anything sporty when I was seven and yet I loved being in the choir and doing any sort of dance and drama. I think I was wary of sport as it involved making an exhibition of myself, or more importantly, possibly letting other people down.

Sue's mother:
'She was a good little girl, full of life, bubbly, outgoing . . .'

Sue at 35:
'I was really a chatterbox . . . it came across on the television programmes . . . But for some reason, I was a little bit hesitant about making a fool of myself . . . Perhaps that's because I was an only child . . . Most of my friends had brothers and sisters who would stand up for them or look after them if they got into trouble . . . You're very conscious of the fact that you've got to look after yourself . . .'

❝ I didn't feel like going to a grammar school. I just, you know, comprehensive school it just seemed more friendly . . . ❞

I can remember 14 quite well. I was having the time of my life – I loved the school and I was really into boys. My first proper boyfriend was called Jimmy. That was in the first or second year so I was about 12. Jackie had moved to Hainault by then and I used to go down and spend weekends at her house. Jimmy and his friends would all come down there and we'd sit in Jackie's front room playing card games and Murder in the Dark – all good clean fun!

Jackie, Lynn and I passed the 11 Plus and we were all told we could go to grammar school. But Jackie and I wanted to go to St Paul's Way because it was a brand-new school and it had its own swimming pool. And that was it, we just separated. We'd already drifted apart from Lynn a bit because she's quite studious and we were getting a little more rebellious by this time.

Clothes were very important then. I wanted to have the really short skirts, the tights with the holes down the side and the flat boys' brogues. We'd just been through the skinhead phase so we had the suits and the pocket handkerchiefs. That's where Jackie and me differed – she went very hippy and I went very mod.

Sue at 14.

I know The Monkees were on telly then but it's difficult to pin records down to that time. I do remember three of us making up little dance routines. We had this one we used to do to Dionne Warwick's 'Walk On By'. We'd all do the harmonies, 'If you see me walking down the street . . .'

But the biggest thing in my life was drama. I loved it, absolutely loved it. The change in me from seven to 14 was like, you know, when a butterfly comes out, a metamorphosis. You can't be self-conscious if you're going to play Alice in *Alice in Wonderland*! When I first started secondary school we were auditioning and – for some reason and I'll never know why – Miss Ellis said she wanted me to play Alice. I was overwhelmed. From that moment I never looked back, I was in everything. I'm sure I owe that teacher so much towards my self-confidence.

Jackie and me used to do pantomimes at the Town Hall, and we did a professional show at the Toynbee Theatre. Round about 14 we were doing old time music hall songs in old people's homes for Christmas. I remember doing *Oh What a Lovely War* and I had to sing this song, 'I'll Make a Man of Any

One of You'. It was quite a sexy song and I had to go into the audience and sit on their laps, and I think it was about that time that I realised that I was really growing up!

Our drama teacher wanted me to go to drama school and I flirted with the idea but I was too much of a coward I think. Sometimes I wish I had but, you know, at 14 I'd get a lot of stick from the other kids who weren't involved in it. If it's not in your nature you can never explain that to anyone – the thrill of doing something like that, the pleasure it gives you, the sense of achievement. You also get out of a lot of lessons! I also really enjoyed sport by then, especially team games like netball and rounders. I was proud to be in the school teams.

My family moved into a new block of flats when I was about 12. It was only a nine-storey block but we were on the top floor and I remember going through a period of looking down on everything and feeling totally cut off. The flat had central heating and a fitted bathroom but there didn't seem to be any neighbours around. I don't remember having friends visiting the flat. I must have gone to their houses.

My dad has always been a bit of a practical joker. He's a really good man, always happy. When you're a young kid it doesn't matter – he trips you up as you walk past – but when you get into your teens little things like that tend to aggravate you. It must have been when I was around 14 when the jokes started to wind me up. I'd say to Mum, 'Make him stop doing that!' I always thought of Mum as a friend and I knew I could go to her if I was particularly worried or upset about something.

Sue at 14, on television:
'I like serials – I like *Peyton Place* and *Crossroads*.'

On travel:
'I have [been abroad]. Spain, Gibraltar and Casablanca. That was interesting, that.'

On boyfriends:
'That's personal, ain't it? . . . We shan't tell him, shall we?'

On money:
'It does mean a lot to us now, with the clothes and the new fashions and everything, doesn't it? Midis and that – you need money.'

On rich people:
'I don't see why they should have the luck when people work all their lives and haven't got half as much as they have. It doesn't seem fair.'

On being rich:
'I don't mind. I'd like to stay as I am. I don't want to be too rich. I don't want to be too poor.'

On God:
'Well, if you're brought up to believe in him, you do.'

On marriage:
'I don't think I'd get married too early. I'd like to have a full life first, and meet people . . . before you commit yourself to a family.'

On what she wanted out of life:
'Just to be content with what I'm doing and be happy with it, and to know where I'm going.'

Sue at 14.

Sue's mother:
'We used to love to go and see her in her drama . . . I remember her in *Oh What a Lovely War*. She came on singing on her own, which took a bit of nerve . . . Her nan was so proud.'

'She was pretty sensible but I used to tell her to have respect for herself where the boys were concerned . . . She used to come to me and I'd try to advise her.'

Sue at 35:
'. . . at 14 I remember every time they asked a question it was always me that answered it. And when I watch it I just cringe because you come out with such rubbish . . . and I'm thinking, "Why is it always you? Why don't you stop and let someone else . . . ?" '

' . . . everything's not that cut and dried. It's not either a career or a family – it's what's in the middle. I mean, am I just going to carry on as I am now . . . and end up on the shelf? Or am I just going to get married? Could be any day . . . '

Sue at 21.

At 21 I was the only one who wasn't married and every single press cutting has got that remark I made about how I might end up on the shelf. If you say anything remotely interesting they tend to keep repeating it. And I can't believe I said it because I was having the time of my life, I really was. I know it might sound conceited but I didn't dream for one minute I'd end up on the shelf. Sometimes I think you say anything rather than leave an empty space, because someone asks you a question and you're on the telly.

After school, I worked for a local bank, then I moved to an insurance firm in the City. They actually made us all redundant because they moved to Devon. I was engaged to Keith at the time. He was lovely. Broke my mum's heart, it did, when I split up with him. I think I outgrew him a bit. I don't know. We were quite young, I must have been 17 or 18, that sort of age.

So then I went to work for this travel firm, where I used to arrange group trips as incentives for firms. For example, they'd run a promotion and they'd send their 100 best salesmen to the South of France for a conference. We'd make the flight bookings, look after them, arrange the entertainment or whatever. I was a secretary but I did get to go on one or two of the trips. In fact we were all booked to go to the South of France one year but there was an air strike so we had to go to Aviemore instead – I was gutted! Actually it was good – a real experience. I took a friend with me, we all had smart uniforms, and we acted as couriers. At 21 I left the travel firm to work in Spain for the summer. I did that for two years. It was great, the best time of my life. I used to hand out cards outside clubs to get people to go in – they call it 'propping'! I went out with a group of friends, we found a cheap pension, and I got a few little jobs, just to tide me over. Sometimes there'd be 40 of us and we'd all go to the beach and have our own party. One or two of them would bring their guitars and we used to have wonderful times.

The first year I went to Spain some of us had this job at a very expensive club. We'd have to dance until 11 or 12 o'clock so the place would look busy. We didn't actually get paid, we'd get free drinks instead. We were so wrapped up in our own social circle that we never met any of the tourists. We'd just have our drinks, have a good time and then go back to our own crowd.

I met my husband Bill just after they made *21*. By that time I was working as an Editorial Secretary for the Library Association. They actually gave me two months holiday the following year to go to Spain for the second time.

While I was at the Library Association I was also working a couple of evenings a week in a pub. I've always found it very easy to talk to people and I love the atmosphere in pubs. Anyway, that's where I met Bill. I knew him from when we were very young – we'd been to the same school – but he was a couple of years older than me. I recognised him when he came in and a friend said, 'Don't get too friendly with him because he's going to Spain, he goes there every year.' I said, 'Well, so am I,' and we ended up doing a lot of our early courting in Spain.

I really was very happy at 21. I had a good job, a great social life, I was happy at home and there was always lots of trust between me and my parents. Everyone's got their own little secrets but I could always be fairly honest with my mum because she's quite broadminded.

Sue at 21, on money:
'It's foolish to get depressed over money.'

Sue

On Jackie's wedding:
'I was pleased I was there. It seemed the right place to be. I mean, I was glad I was at her wedding. I've known her a long while.'

On marriage:
'Marriage didn't appeal to me. I've still got my ideals . . . I don't know what it's all about, obviously, so I've still got pictures of cosy evenings indoors.'

Sue's mother:
'She loved her job at the travel agent. She didn't say she'd never get married but she wasn't rushing into it . . . She seemed very contented.'

Sue at 35:
'It was about this time that I started worrying about what the next programme would be called. It must have hit me that my age was never going to be a well-kept secret!'

' It was hard first of all when I gave up work –
from having a fairly high salary to nothing was
hard. But you get used to it. Whatever your
circumstances are, you live in them. You get
used to them and you cope. Everybody does. '

Billy and I got married when I was 24. It was a big church wedding, the
business, you know. Wonderful really, for somebody who likes to be in the
limelight. We went to Kos, a Greek island, for our honeymoon. And I loved
being part of Bill's family – he's got two sisters and a brother.

I was still working for the Library Association then and Billy was a gas
fitter. We got a council flat and nearly a year later I fell pregnant with
William. He was born in the February and he looked so much like Billy – he
really was the spitting image of him. The only trouble was I couldn't feed
him myself. I really tried but it just didn't work and I used to sob all the time
in the hospital. He thrived anyway on the bottle and it wasn't the end of the
world but I so wanted to be the perfect mother.

I can remember the first couple of months curling up in a foetal position
on the settee when my mum went home. I was terrified of being on my own
with a newborn baby, even though I loved him to pieces. I mean, I'd never
had any brothers or sisters with babies that I'd been used to holding or
changing or anything like that.

Mum was really good. She came round more or less every day. I'd
damaged a nerve in my back during the delivery and I had a sort of delayed
reaction. It took me months to walk normally – I used to drag one of my feet
behind because the pain in my lower back was so bad. I'd push the big pram,
dragging one leg behind me, like the Hunchback of Notre Dame!

When we had William I gave up work and I know it's silly but I couldn't
stand not having my own money. In the same breath I was really adamant
that I didn't want to go to work when I had a child. I had a Saturday job in
a building society but that was only a couple of hours so I didn't really
consider it working. I used to go to playgroups and one o'clock clubs but
basically my personality doesn't revolve around young children. I hated the
sleepless nights. I've met hundreds of women who feel the same way but some
just seem to be able to cope with it better than others. It used to depress me.

Billy helped at home. I used to be in a ladies darts team and he would look after William while I played darts on a Monday night. But, even so, little cracks started appearing in the marriage. Probably a lot of it was down to us both being sociable people. I really missed going out and I think it just eats away at you and then you start getting resentful, indoors alone.

Just after they made *28 Up* I discovered I was pregnant with Kathryn. Even though I wasn't actually pregnant when they made the programme, in my eyes I looked like I was. It took me years to get out of that motherhood mode because I always knew I'd want more than one. So it was never a case of, well I've had my child and now I'm going to get myself back in shape. I was waiting, in a sort of limbo.

Sue at 28, on her life:

'I'm lucky, I expect, because I still manage to do my own thing. I've got a husband who lets me do what I want and a mum who helps me out.'

Sue at 28.

On her education:

'My mum . . . knew I could go to grammar . . . I decided that I didn't want to and she encouraged me in the choice that I made. And, right or wrong, that was my choice, as much as I was capable of making a decision. And I enjoyed myself . . . you can only have regrets about things if you're not happy with the way you are.'

On herself, Jackie and Lynn:

'I think that we all could have gone any way we wanted to . . . within our capabilities. I mean – we were able to choose our own jobs quite freely.'

On marriage:

'I think that to get married young there must be things that you miss. You must miss that crucial state of being yourself because the minute you get married you're no longer a single being – you're a partnership and that should be the idea behind it.'

On having children:

'I think there's still a lot of pressure put on young married couples to have children, as though it's expected of them, and I think it's all wrong. It's just a personal decision that everyone's entitled to make, and knowing what it does to your life I can completely understand someone who decides not to.'

Sue's mother:

'When William was first born Sue had her worries. But she was always a very good mother – very organised and efficient. Some women can breeze through it but not many. You're thrust in at the deep end. She coped, and as he got older she got better at it.'

Sue at 35:

'At 28 I wasn't happy with myself at all. I wasn't happy about the way I looked, the way I came across. The programme was fine, it didn't embarrass me particularly . . . I just wasn't happy.'

Don't let them call it *35 Up* - there must be a kinder way. All these years I've been making out I was 28! It's funny but the programme is so much a part of my life that I can't imagine what it'd be like without it. And I couldn't ever refuse to take part because it would be like – sacrilege. It's terrifying but it's also exciting. And I think there's a part of me that thrives on anything that's exciting. But it is really quite scary. You think, what have I done? It makes you aware of the circumstances you're in and you think, what do I want to admit to, what do I want to keep private?

I'm happy now and yet I don't feel that I've made a success of the last seven years, because if your marriage has failed then in my book that's not a successful thing to happen. I separated from Billy just over three years ago. Kathryn was nearly two when we decided to split and it was quite friendly as splits go. He moved back with his mum and I stayed here with the kids. He comes round and takes the kids out on Sunday mornings and, up until a couple of months ago, he had them on Monday nights when I went out to darts.

We're still friends, we've never been ones for arguing anyway. I've never bad-mouthed him and I know he wouldn't do it to me. If we can't be married then we've got to go for the next best thing, which is to be good friends.

When we broke up William was five and I explained to him as best I could. I just said, 'You know how Kathryn sometimes gets on your nerves, you fight, she annoys you. Well, that's how me and Daddy were. We used to get on each other's nerves, so we decided that we'd be better friends if we lived in separate houses.' You don't really know what's going on in their minds but I think he's accepted it quite well. And I think the way we are has a lot to do with it.

Sue at work in the building society.

Billy and I never had any strong feelings against each other anyway, we just had nothing in common. We were hardly talking, and you can't just drift like that for ever. Years ago no marriage would have ended for a reason like that. But these days women expect so much more out of a marriage. It's not just that they won't put up with being badly treated, it's that they won't put up with not being happy. And nowadays you can take the risk because you know you're never going to starve, you don't have to rely on anybody else's wage. You can be self-sufficient.

So many of my friends are single parents. It's almost like an exclusive club because we all help each other out. One of my best friends is Bill's sister Diane, who has been separated from her husband for four years. She has two children round about the same age as mine, and we go on holiday together every year.

Sue with Kathryn and William.

My Mum and Dad have always been there for me and for each other. They're a very loving couple – very reliable and wonderful. I mean, we're not a particularly gushy family but you couldn't ask for a better Mum and Dad really. And they're both so good with the kids.

William's eight now. He's handsome – still the spitting image of his Dad. He's not very sporty, except for swimming and snooker, and he loves reading, especially encyclopedias, the *Guinness Book of Records*, things like that. He's always getting into new hobbies, collecting things. He could read when he was five and I don't think I ever taught him how, he just seemed to do it on his own. He takes after me for his love of books. He isn't a rough, tough lad and also like me he hasn't much of a temper. But I've said to him, 'You're going to have to look after yourself out there, kid. You're on your own.'

Kathryn is different. She's five now and a little firebrand. She's lovely, my Miss Personality. I wanted a girl so badly and I was so happy when she was born. She came out screaming, and she's been screaming ever since! If she falls over she screams so loud that I've had perfect strangers coming from streets away to see what's happened!

Billy often used to babysit for the kids after we split, but things change and it's not always convenient these days. There's no one in my life at the moment. There was someone special but it didn't work out. I'm afraid of actually living with somebody again, because I quite like living on my own. I like to be able to do things on the spur of the moment and when you're on your own you're the only one making the decisions. I don't think it's an ideal way to bring up kids. And it is hard work. But you don't think about the hard work because it becomes a way of life. You also have to like your own company, as you spend many evenings alone. Thank goodness for TV and video!

I've just started a part-time job in a building society and now Mum's working too, so I have to pick up the kids after school. It's really hard to manage. Before this I was on Income Support. Once you've been on this a while it's very hard to get away from it – I think they call it the poverty trap. You don't have to worry about paying your rent and poll tax as a single parent on Income Support – you have other money worries when you're on your own with kids! It's hard to leave that security behind and go back into part-time employment.

If I went full-time I'd be fine but I'd have to find a job that paid well enough for me to pay someone to pick them up for me and mind them on school holidays. The job would have to be so well paid and it would be so time-consuming that I really don't think I'm ready for that yet. The truth is that I don't want to be a full-time worker and a part-time Mum. I want to be able to pick the kids up from school. Even working part-time you've got a problem with school holidays, although in my area we're lucky to have play centres which look after them during most school breaks.

Going back to work is a bit nerve-racking because I'll have to pay all my own bills and they won't tell you what sort of rent rebate you may get until you can send in wage slips. It's very difficult to work out a budget when you have to *start* work before you know where you stand. I may be fractionally better off but I don't know yet. It's like a vicious circle but the way I look at it, if you want to get on, if you want to change your life, you've got to get on the ladder somewhere. A lot of my friends said, 'Do it, do it. Get on there because, although you might not be better off now, sooner or later you will be.'

Looking back over the last 28 years, I sometimes wish I'd gone on the stage, only because I still remember how much I enjoyed it. And I see people on the telly and I think, well they're only people like me. They all did it, they had the nerve, they took a chance. And I wasn't prepared to, basically.

Where would I like to be in another seven years? I'd like to move out of the East End – for the kids' sake, not particularly for mine because I actually quite like it here. I love having friends around me and at my age I'm past worrying about where I live and whether it's green. But for the kids I'd love to move out – not far, Kent, Essex, that sort of area. At the moment it's practically impossible to make the break – I don't own my own home. I still live in a council house.

Now William's coming up to the age where I've got to think about secondary schools for him. And I don't know what I'm going to do because, in my opinion, there aren't many really good schools round here. I'd send him to a private school if I could afford it – I only wish we could move out before he had to go to secondary school.

I'd like to see myself settled again one day because I think the novelty of being a single parent is starting to wear off a bit. I couldn't face living on my own forever. It's hard taking someone else into your life, especially when you've got kids, but people do make a success of it. You also have to find someone willing to take on two children. I'm not saying it's going to be easy, if it happens. Who knows? One thing I do know is that nothing stays the same, and a lot can happen in seven years.

I'd like to be working full-time before too long because basically I'm not one for scrimping and I've always been a worker. I consider that my job has been as a mum for the last eight years and I've enjoyed it, being here for them. But I've not enjoyed doing without certain things. I'd hate anyone to think that the kids were missing out on anything. I mean, they're doing all right. But I know there's always more you can do.

Sue's mother:
'Now she's at a sort of crossroads in her life. Her marriage is over and she's trying to start again. It's a trauma but she realises she's more or less standing on her own. I know she has days when she feels a bit down . . . but she always manages to fight back . . . She always tries – she doesn't sit back and wait for things to happen.'

William, Kathryn and Sue.

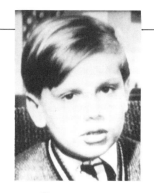

JOHN

'When I leave this school I'm going to Colet Court and then I will be going to Westminster Boarding School, if I pass the exam. And then we think I'm going to Cambridge and Trinity Hall.'

When John was seven he was going to Wagners, a pre-prep school in Kensington, London. His father was a steel consultant. John's mother is former editor of *The World Today*, the monthly journal of the Royal Institute of International Affairs, and comes from Bulgaria. In fact she is the great-granddaughter of the first prime minister of Bulgaria, and the granddaughter of another. John has one brother, Stephen, who was 12, and a sister, Tania, one. When John was seven, the family lived in Kensington.

John at 7, on poor children:
'I don't think much of the accents . . . but it doesn't prevent me liking them.'

John (*centre*) with his mother and elder brother, Stephen.

On schools:
'I think it's not a bad idea to pay for schools because if we didn't schools would be so nasty and crowded.'

On The Beatles:
'I just loathe their haircuts.'

On newspapers:
'I read the *Observer* and *The Times* . . . I usually look at the headlines and then read about them.'

On girls:
'. . . when boys go round with girls they don't pay attention to what they're doing. Yes, my grandmother had an accident because a boyfriend was kissing his girlfriend in the street.'

On the other children at the *7 Up* party:
'Well, some of them were rather dirty.'

6 I think it's just about the best place you can live your life, in England . . . I think the parliamentary system is agreeable, to me at least. And that's about it. One's free in England. **9**

At14 John was a weekly boarder at Westminster School. He wasn't sure what he wanted to do after university but thought he might try law. He had two dreams: one, to be a concert pianist; the other, to be a Conservative politician. In his spare time he enjoyed going to art galleries, walking and reading, especially the Russian classics. He didn't have a girlfriend. John lost his father very suddenly at the age of nine. When he was 14 his mother was still living in Kensington.

John at 14, on his education:
'. . . when you board on a weekly basis you have the best of both worlds, so to speak. One sees one's parents at the weekend and one gets all the benefits from an English boarding school.'

'We have about ten pianos and practice rooms and there are choral societies and two choirs . . .'

On pocket money:
'[I get] 8 shillings a week . . . I usually spend very little at school. I collect stamps and I spend quite a lot on that.'

On travel:
'I've been to so many places – Sicily, Italy, France and Spain, and Switzerland many times.'

On religion:
'That's a difficult question to answer. I just do [believe in God]. It's either a yes or no question.'

On politics:
'I'd have voted Conservative . . . The Conservatives will do the best for the country.'

On racial discrimination:
'It's rather vile . . . So is any kind of discrimination of a basic nature that you can't change . . . I couldn't care less whether people are discriminated against . . . because they're nasty or selfish or anything. But, I mean, one can't help one's colour.'

On strikes:
'It's very irresponsible because we all want more money, as much money as we can get. And what would happen if we all stopped working just because we wanted more money?'

'I wouldn't allow any strikes . . . I would set up a tribunal where workers could apply for better wages and this tribunal would have the final word and if it said no wage rise, no wage rise . . . It seems to me iniquitous that people should be paid when they're not doing any work, which is what the unions do . . . It's not that they wouldn't still be able to ask for more money, but they wouldn't be able to strike for it, which . . . is so damaging.'

On class:
'I think . . . the differences that used to separate the classes have diminished greatly. I mean, when one was a duke one used to be set above everybody else but now, look at the Duke of . . . !'

On girls:
'I think they are still bores for the most part.'

On wanting to be a concert pianist:
'I think there's too much competition nowadays. There are so many good pianists and only a few make the grade . . .'

John at 14.

On his ambition:
'[I'm ambitious for] fame and power . . . political power.'

On why he wanted to be rich:
'. . . because I don't want to be tied down to the dullness of an everyday job. I want to be able to have enough money so I can indulge in things that interest me, like collecting paintings . . .'

On himself:
'I'm a bit more reactionary than most . . . I like tradition.'

'Well, I mean one grows so steadily that one never notices. I feel the same as I felt at seven. I may not be.'

6 If I believe my principles are right, that I'm doing the right thing to bring my children up by them, then it won't matter to me if I'm living in the Middle Ages mentally, I shall do what's right. 9

After leaving Westminster John did a month's training at Sandhurst. He spent nine months in the regular army – in the Cavalry – and was posted first to Cyprus and then to Germany. At 21 he was in his third year reading Law on a scholarship at Christ Church College, Oxford, and hadn't decided whether or not he wanted to rejoin his regiment after university. He was also considering possible careers in merchant banking, the law or politics.

John loved being at Oxford, and had a busy social life – with house parties most weekends – and plenty of girlfriends. He played tennis in the summer and went beagling twice a week in the winter. Christ Church had its own pack of hounds – the dogs would sniff out the hare and the beaglers would follow on foot. John always loved horses and one of his ambitions at the time was to buy his own hunter.

At 21 he had travelled widely and spoke fluent French and German. He was still a fine pianist, if a bit rusty, and enjoyed all sorts of music though he'd never bought a pop record. He said he'd like to marry young and saw himself with a big house and lots of children.

John at 21, on privilege:
'I can't see there's anything wrong as long as people don't abuse the opportunities and privileges they have. If people behave responsibly then I think it's very good – there's a sort of stability and structure in society.'

'I think that anyone who goes to a really good school has had a leg-up. But I mean . . . if I'd missed exams at my school and had to go to a grotty public school I wouldn't have thought it any advantage at all.'

'All this talk about opportunities, it's something I did slightly object to in the programme, in that we were shown, at the age of seven, outlining the academic . . . career that most of us did in fact pursue. Each sentence ended up . . . "John *is* at Westminster, Andrew *is* at Charterhouse . . ." It implied that we just sailed through . . . It didn't show the sleepless nights, the sort of poring over our books, you know, all the sweat and toil that got us to university. It was presented as if it was just . . . part of some indestructible birthright . . . It didn't show us having to do beastly jobs in the holidays . . . to make ends meet . . . It didn't give a very real sort of impression.'

On education:
'I do believe parents have a right to educate their children as they think fit. And I think someone who works on an assembly line at some of these car factories and earning a huge wage can well afford to send their children to private school if they wanted to. Just because some . . . people perhaps don't put that as high on their priorities as having a smart car or something.'

On class:
'I do believe in a sort of ordered and structured society . . . Some people have better times than others but, you know, it doesn't mean because you sweep the streets you are any less valuable than someone who is running a huge corporation. I mean, not everyone can be at the top. As long as people are happy in what they're doing . . .'

John at 21.

On Oxford:
'Well, first of all, it's such a beautiful place. There's more to it than just swotting away at one's books. I think it's very difficult not to get something out of it. There's such a sort of atmosphere of culture and timelessness about the place that I think you do . . . mature an awful lot.'

On a career in the law:
'If I go to the Bar I should like a reasonable amount of success. I shouldn't like to be on the breadline . . .'

'It's hard work but . . . when you get to a certain eminence you take the work you want and you take the holidays you want and you don't really dance to anyone's tune, all of which quite suits me.'

On his political ambitions:
'I'd quite like to go into politics, but that's easier said than done.'

On social changes:

'I believe people who . . . go on a lot about the permissive society are missing the point if they think that the only thing that is wrong is sex. I think, you know, decreasing respect for the family as a unit, increasing dishonesty in business . . . I mean, there used to be . . . much stronger developed ideas of commercial integrity . . . Nowadays people seem to be really sort of out for themselves.'

On people who leave England:

'I can't say I really approve of the sorts of people who emigrate . . . I do think . . . people who've had things and gained well from them really ought to stay and help the country out when, you know, things aren't going very well. I don't believe in all this pulling one's money out . . . people should have the right to live where they like and also to move their assets around, but on a moral level I really feel quite strongly that people shouldn't quit.'

'I think the more you have out of the country, the more privileges you are born with, the greater your duty is.'

After leaving Oxford John was called to the Bar at 24, after just over a year as a pupil. He went into Chambers in Lincoln's Inn, specialising in company law. Although he had to put in very long hours he found the work stimulating and rewarding.

At 28 he was living with his mother during the week and he also had a weekend cottage in Oxfordshire. He still voted Tory, he was driving a Renault 5 and enjoyed going to the cinema and the opera. He had just announced his engagement.

John did not wish to be interviewed for *28 Up*.

John and Claire on their wedding day.

John still enjoys his work at the Chancery Bar, dividing his time between his house in West London and a farm on which he and his wife now live in Northamptonshire. He has developed a passion for gardening, and spends most of his weekends digging the herbaceous borders. He has recently resumed playing the piano after years of neglect and – in line with his aspirations at the age of 14 – has begun to collect paintings.

AT 35

At the time of going to press, he is actively involved with others in setting up a charity designed to channel aid to Bulgaria, where (as in Romania) the material situation has deteriorated substantially during the death throes of the Communist régime. He has for the time being shelved any political ambitions. Five and a half years ago he married Claire, elder daughter of Sir Donald Logan, a former ambassador to Bulgaria.

John at 35.

John on his farm in Northamptonshire.

John and Claire.

ANDREW

❛ When I leave this school I go to Broadstairs, St Peter's Court. Then . . . to Charterhouse and after that to Trinity Hall, Cambridge. **❜**

I was brought up in South Kensington in London in a tall, rather grand-looking, Victorian white-painted house with pillars on either side of the front door. My father was a merchant banker in the City and for many years also wrote a daily City column for a newspaper in the evenings. He was born in Austria and came to England as a boy with his family just before the War. My mother, who was also born and spent her early years abroad, in France, had at one time a small beauty and hairdressing salon in the West End, which was more of a hobby than a serious business venture. I remember as a small child of ten going there after school and being fascinated by all the exotic-looking people who passed through its doors.

Until I started full-time school, my parents had a nanny to help look after me. It wasn't the old-fashioned sort of arrangement, where the parents would only see their child at the most once a day, but more like a mother's help. Perhaps surprisingly, I don't really remember anything about my nannies. I suppose this is because one doesn't generally remember that far back. That thought sometimes makes me wonder whether, if I were to fall under a bus tomorrow, my own children, who are now two and five, would remember me when they were grown-up.

I don't have any brothers or sisters and, perhaps partly to make up for this, pets, particularly dogs, always played an important part in my childhood. I spent many happy hours taking a succession of large family dogs for walks and playing with them in the garden.

Although we lived in central London, my parents were both very keen on the countryside and from quite early on we used to spend the weekends in a small cottage that they rented in a very rural part of Sussex. It was marvellous for a small boy to be able to get out in the open spaces at the weekends and do all the things that you cannot do in London, and I have loved the country ever since. This is a feeling that my wife, Jane, shares. Although, because of my job, we live in Wimbledon on the outskirts of London, as soon as we could possibly afford it after getting married, we bought an old barn, also in Sussex, which we are in the process of converting, and to which we try and escape most weekends. It is nice to see now that our own children seem to enjoy going down to the country as much as I did as a child.

When I was seven, after the making of the first programme, I was sent away to a boys' boarding school in Broadstairs, Kent. This was in a large, rambling Victorian pile with an air of faded grandeur which, like so many similar institutions, was later pulled down to make way for a housing estate. It was run by a headmaster who must have been in his early sixties and his mother, and its main claim to fame was that many years previously a member of the Royal Family had been educated there.

Andrew in 1966.

Andrew at 7, on his school:

'I think the system of having house captains is rather good, because when somebody is naughty the house captain asks him and has a talk to him.'

On his daily routine:

'When I go home I have tea, then I practise my piano, then I practise my recorder and then I start watching television . . . I have my bath at six o'clock and then go to bed at seven and read until half past seven.'

On girls:

'. . . the girls never do what the boys want . . . they always start playing with dolls when the boys want to play rough and tumble . . . And they always take you away from whatever game you're playing yourself.'

On newspapers:

'I read the *Financial Times* . . . I like my newspaper because I've got shares in it and I know every day what the shares are. On Mondays they don't move up so I don't look at it.'

On the other children at the *7 Up* party:
'I played with them really quite naturally. I think they were rather nice really.'

Andrew at 35:
'Although, with hindsight, the education I received there [at boarding school in Kent] was to stand me in good stead for the future, I did not really enjoy being away from home at that age and I do not think that I would want to send my own sons away from home at such a tender age.'

6 ... we're not necessarily typical examples and I think that's what people seeing the programme might think and falsely. I mean, they tend to typecast us. So everything we say, they will think, that's a typical result of public schools. **9**

Andrew during the filming of *Seven Plus Seven*.

Following boarding school in Kent, I went to a public school, Charterhouse in Surrey, which I generally enjoyed. Although we were encouraged to try and do well, it was not too pressured academically. Discipline, though, was fairly strict, and caning by the headmaster still an accepted practice. I experienced this first-hand at the age of 15, when I managed to get hold of a bottle of vodka from a local off-licence and disgraced myself by drinking too much and being sick out of the dormitory window on to the housemaster's lawn. I have disliked vodka ever since.

When I was in my mid teens the school arranged a series of aptitude tests designed to help assess our chances of going to university and what career might suit us best. In my case the results indicated that I was unlikely to make the grade for university, or at least for any university that I would wish to go to, and the career that would suit me best would be hotel management.

During my last year at Charterhouse, my parents separated and then got divorced. The divorce itself seemed a very civilised affair, with no squabbling over money or custody of children. Although each of my parents have since remarried, they still remain good friends and regularly speak to each other.

Andrew at 14, on boarding school:
'Well, I think boarding makes you feel self-sufficient and also it teaches you to be away from your parents, and to live with people for a long time, which you have to do in later life anyway.'

On girls:
'Beginning to become more important . . . they are no longer just bores . . .'

On poor people:
'When I went to Glasgow and saw the Gorbals, that rather upset me . . . to think that people are living in that state when we waste things every day.'

On money:
'[I'd like to be rich] . . . mainly to be self sufficient, to feel that you don't have to owe anything to anybody.'

On racial discrimination:
'I think both black and white are equal.'

On religion:
'You have got to believe in something so God seems to be the most logical thing.'

Andrew at 35:
'Because of my age and the fact that I was living away from home most of the time . . . [my parents' divorce] did not seem to have a great impact on my life except for the practical aspects of having to go to different places to visit each of my parents. It did, however, perhaps have a greater effect later when it made me think particularly carefully before taking the plunge and getting married myself.'

Andrew at 16.

AT 21

❝ I'd like to be a solicitor and also fairly successful . . . After I've qualified as a solicitor then I'll have to rethink . . . I don't know at all what will happen after that. **❞**

Slightly to my own surprise, I managed to pass the necessary exams to go to Cambridge (one of the papers involved writing a three-hour essay on the subject 'If silence is golden then what is noise?'). After a short time spent travelling round Europe and working at various odd jobs, I went up to Trinity College to read Law.

Although the course there was very demanding, it was a marvellous place to be in one's early twenties. Unlike public school, Cambridge had a complete cross-section of people of different backgrounds and with different interests, and I made a number of enduring friendships during my time there.

After leaving university, I went to law college for a brief period and joined a large City law firm in London, where I was made a partner a couple of years ago and have remained since.

Andrew at 21, on himself and John at 7:
'Well, we didn't know very much when we were seven, but we were still funny . . . certainly I was a fairly precocious little brat . . .'

On equality of opportunity:
'We've been taught to expect more, not that because we've been to private schools we're better qualified necessarily. It's a matter of expectations.'

On education:
'I think if people earn their money they should have the right to spend it and education is very important . . . you can never be sure of leaving your children any worldly goods, but at least you can be sure that once you've given them a good education that's something that no one can take away.'

Andrew at 21.

> **'**I've had all the material advantages and I've had the opportunity to make the most of them . . . I have been really lucky. **,**

AT 28

I met my wife Jane when I was in my mid twenties. A friend had asked me to be usher at his wedding near Crowborough in Sussex, and Jane was there as his cousin. I don't know whether it was love at first sight but I do remember that, at the time, I had an extremely unreliable old Triumph which kept on breaking down in the most embarrassing places, and being greatly impressed by the fact that Jane never seemed to complain when all the drivers around us were hooting and swearing. She was also extremely good at pushing the car to get it started again!

Jane lived with her parents in Yorkshire and, after we had been seeing each other at weekends for some months, slightly to the shock of her parents, she gave up her home and job to come and be with me in London. We were married two years later.

Andrew during the filming of *28 Up*

Andrew at 28.

Andrew at 28, on being a solicitor:
'Well, you have to have a legal ability in my business, obviously. And you have to have a sort of bedside manner as far as clients are concerned. It is no good being brilliant if you can't really communicate with your clients.'

On education:
'First of all there is the argument that people should have the choice if they have earned the money to spend it. Then the other argument is that if we all went to the same sort of schools, those schools would probably be better because those people who had influence would do their utmost to make sure they were better if they had to send their children there . . . I think probably the latter choice is fairly impractical so I suppose one has to continue with the idea of everyone having a choice.'

On equality of opportunity:
'It's a shame that all people can't get the opportunities that I have had. And I'm not sure how one deals with that.'

Jane:

'Andrew didn't go for a haughty deb, he went for a good Yorkshire lass. But . . . obviously he knew what he wanted . . . I think I'm probably quite down to earth. I tend to be less extravagant than some women . . .'

AT 35

Our first son, Alexander, was born in 1985 and our second, Timothy, two and a half years later. Inevitably our lives now are very much centred round the children. Jane, who had previously been working as a secretary, decided that she would not go back to work after our first son was born, and she has her hands pretty full looking after them.

We can all find something to complain about from time to time, but when all is said and done, I realise how fortunate I have been. My main wish now is to give my children the same opportunities that I have had – to give them a good start. It is then up to them what they make of their lives.

Andrew at 35.

Andrew, Jane, Alexander and Timothy (*front*).

Andrew with Jane and their two sons,
Alexander (*left*) and Timothy.

NICK

' When I grow up I'd like to find out all about the moon and all that. '

By the time I was seven we were in the same farmhouse in the Yorkshire Dales that my parents are living in now. I think I was happy there. It was a fairly big, ramshackle farmhouse with thick limestone walls that were crumbly. In fact some of the walls crumbled rather more than you might like – my bedroom had a hole at one point that went all the way through to the outside.

The kitchen had this sink that was literally carved out of stone, it was made of granite. And there was one of those farmhouse-type stoves in the corner, where there was always something cooking. Next to the kitchen there was a stairway and then at the front of the house there were a couple of fairly big sitting rooms, one that we used all the time and one for special occasions. At the top of the stairs there were three bedrooms and a bathroom, a couple of little bedrooms and a whacking great big one.

In some ways, as I commented at the time, going into a city was very exciting to me, because it was so terribly different. My father's a farmer and he spent the whole time trying to scrape a living out of sheep and cows, I guess. I don't remember having much of an opinion about living on the farm. The farm was just something that was there.

It wasn't altogether great being the only kid around. I think my best friend – I don't know if this was at seven or a little bit older – was a 15-year-old who came to work for my father. He was the nearest person to my age around and so I sort of trailed along after him and I was terribly upset when he finished his apprenticeship and got another job.

My main memories of around that time would probably be of going to

Nick holding his brother Andrew.

school in Arncliffe. I didn't like school much. I mean, I didn't mind lessons but I didn't like maths – I didn't like add-ups and take-aways and long division. And I never liked playtime. I wished the teachers wouldn't send us out because all we did was fight. I was the only child in my village and I didn't really know how to interact with other little kids very well. So playtime was . . . well, it wasn't awful, but it wasn't great.

I think, even at that age, I read a lot. When I was very tiny, years before that, I'd been running down the centre of the village with a toy dinosaur in my hand and one of the ladies leant over a garden wall and said, 'What have you got, Nicky?' And I told her that it was a Dimetrodon or something. I was way pre-school but I was interested in that sort of thing; aeroplanes and outer space, and all sorts of things.

I remember distinctly my brother Andrew being brought home and the fact that he had these very bright pink legs, and I thought this was very strange. I was very concerned about him.

Nick at 7, on his life:
'I'm the only child in the village except for my baby brother. He was one last Friday, I mean the Friday before last Friday.'

On children from the town:
'They'd like to come out for a holiday in the country . . . I'd like to have a holiday in the town.'

On coloured people:
'I've only seen them on television and places like that.'

On whether he had a girlfriend:
'I don't want to answer that. I don't answer those kind of questions.'

On how he'd change the world:
'If I could change the world, I'd change it into a diamond.'

Nick at 35:
'I think I must have been a rather lonely little boy. I mean . . . I've only really realised quite recently . . . that I was only able to relate to adults, and not to other kids . . . and how it affected my life for quite a long time.'

‘ I've been to Leeds a couple of times. I haven't been to Manchester. I went to London when . . . you made the first programme, but that's the only time I've been. ’

AT 14

When I was 10 I was sent to board at a local grammar school. It was only 15 miles away from home, but in their infinite wisdom the Education Authority decided that it was too far for me to travel each day so I got put in the boarding house. And this seemed perfectly natural to my parents because they'd both been boarders and thought it was OK. Also, from my father's point of view, he thought it would be quite nice for me because I wouldn't have to do jobs around the farm and there would be other kids around.

I will never forget the scene the day I arrived there. I was put in this little dormitory and my parents were standing there, I had this big trunk and all these strange people were milling around. And then they said, 'OK, we'd better go then. Bye bye.' And they went! I know lots of people go to boarding schools at a much younger age, but I didn't like it one bit.

There were three groups in the boarding house. There were the farm kids, who were, broadly speaking, fairly sane and normal. There were Forces kids, some of whom were sane and some who were, you know, a bit over the top. And then there was the third and smallest group, the kids who had been taken away from their parents for one reason or another and put in this boarding school to get them away from whatever was troubling them.

At 14 I still disliked being a boarder. There's a Yorkshire saying, 'You can't do right for doing wrong,' and it was certainly true in the boarding house. Whenever you bumped into any of the teachers you were always doing something wrong, so you were always in trouble. Basically we were like rats in an overcrowded maze. We didn't have anything to do so we were all just picking on each other the whole time.

I worked hard academically. It was easy enough but I was trying hard because there were some very bright kids around who I was competing with.

A couple of times I got into trouble but I don't think I ever did anything really naughty. At 14 or 15 a bunch of us would decide we were 'going over the wall'. This just meant that we'd go down to the town in the middle of the afternoon. Once one of the teachers spotted us trekking through a parking lot and told the teacher on duty. I played it dumb and said I was going to the

Nick with his youngest brother, Christopher.

Nick at 14.

post office. He just gave the standard response, 'Oh you idiot. Get out of my sight, boy.'

Every time I had to go back to school for the start of a new term my dad would drive me back and it was quite poignant in a way. We'd always have had a fairly emotional day because none of us were very happy about me going back. There'd just be me and Dad in the Land Rover, creaking down these roads. And my dad and I, we don't really have a good mechanism for expressing emotion to each other, but I'd be sitting there thinking, 'I'm being dropped off, I'm going to miss my dad . . .' And he'd be saying to me, 'Why don't you give rugby a try?' And he just kept bringing this up.

Eventually I decided if that was what he wanted me to do, then I better had. Up till then I'd been in what they called the rugby sets, the lowest of the low, where we played like a big flock of sheep and there was one huge maul, where you were all standing up wrestling for the ball. But on this particular occasion I remember deciding that, instead of just standing there watching, I was going to try and get the ball out of this heap of bodies. And I found that once I'd started trying I actually could, if I wanted to. So after a while – even though I had absolutely no skill – I got bumped up to playing for the school. When I was 15 I played for Yorkshire Schoolboys and I was immensely proud of this because it was *Yorkshire* and we won all our games. I was the pack leader because I at least could remember the signals!

When I was 14, Christopher, my youngest brother, was three. And we all absolutely adored him. I don't know, but I imagine Andrew felt the same way. I know my parents' lives, since he was born, have been largely devoted to him. I remember being in my first year at the grammar school and standing in the dark in the dormitory, looking out of the window, which was something I shouldn't have been doing because we weren't allowed out of bed. I must have just had the phone conversation with my mother, but it's as if I was talking to her whilst looking out of the window, so I've obviously superimposed the two memories. What she'd been saying on the phone was that Christopher might be deaf.

Nick at 14, on his life:

'In this village there's me and then the next oldest is Andrew there. That's it. I'm not unhappy living on the farm and going to this school and boarding there. It's all right. I think it'd be better than living on the farm all the time. I wouldn't like to live at the school all the time either.'

On whether he had a girlfriend:

'I thought that one would come up, because when I was doing the other one, somebody said, "What do you think about girls?" And I said, "I don't answer questions like that." Is that the reason you are asking me? I thought so. Well, what do you want me to say?'

On religion:

'I'm not sure whether I really believe in God or not. I think to myself, is there a God? And I don't know . . .'

On coloured people:

'I don't care what colour somebody is, unless they're blue, and I think that would be pretty peculiar . . . No, I don't care about colour.'

On poor people:

'I hate poverty for anybody . . . It kind of depresses me.'

On money:

'. . . almost everybody likes money . . . It doesn't give me any pleasure . . . But I certainly don't want to be poor or live in a slum . . .'

On his future:

'I don't think my father wants me to be a farmer . . . I'm not interested in it [farming]. I said I was interested in physics and chemistry. Well, I'm not going to do that here.'

Nick at 35:

'I never seem to learn anything really quickly. I don't have any sort of intuitive ability, particularly with . . . physical activity, and also I think . . . intellectual activities. It takes me a while. I have to . . . sort of think about the process of doing the physical thing and then I can maybe do it.'

AT 21

❛ Well, what have I achieved? I'm not really prepared to accept that I've done anything very special yet . . . I mean, I'm hoping that I might do at some stage, but I don't really think that I've done anything you can call a great success. ❜

Nick at 21.

At 21 I was reading Physics at Merton College, Oxford. The college expected me to get a First but I felt I hadn't been that well prepared at school and I found it a bit of a struggle to begin with. My special interest was nuclear fusion and I was hoping to get some sort of research post eventually. I don't think I was particularly keen on doing research in America at that point.

Oxford wasn't a great place to form and keep relationships, and I used to worry about some of my friends. The ones who were naturally a bit shy often ended up becoming *really* shy. I suppose I had a lot of friends. I used to play rugby for the college and we'd go out boozing a bit, although I only had about £5 spending money a week.

As a student I wasn't very active in politics because I thought the student politicians were a nauseating bunch. I mean, I know that to be a politician you have to go through this, but they were just horribly pretentious. And at Oxford the student politics probably had more to do with class than anything, even if you were going to be a socialist. Of course, all the British prime ministers since God knows when have been at Oxford. I think Callaghan is the only one who didn't go there. A few years before, I used to go to Young Liberals meetings but the Young Liberals at Oxford were kind of ridiculous. It was hard to take them seriously somehow.

My parents were pretty chuffed about me getting into Oxford and they came down once or twice to see it all. I often went back to Yorkshire in the vacations and I'd have to help my father out on the farm.

Nick at 21, on girls:
'The best answer would be to say that I don't answer questions like that . . . It was what I said when I was seven and it's still the most sensible. I mean, what about them!'

On himself:

'I've tried to make a change, yes, a very definite conscious effort not to be shy and to be more outgoing, and this is actually something I can point to in my own past and think – yes, I did make my mind up here, here and here, that I was going to try and change this, this and this. This, being basically my confidence and . . . approach to people in general.'

On having grown up on a farm:

'. . . it's a rather different background to go anywhere – Oxford, perhaps especially. It is a rather more firm foundation I would have thought, as to your character, than being brought up in a city. It's a fixed reference point in a sense – that sort of earthy life and death cycle that you get living on a farm. If something dies, it rots and feeds back into the earth. Sometimes it's helpful in a city, where things that some people are very concerned about seem quite irrelevant.'

On the influence of his father being a farmer:

'. . . a sense of calmness in some situations. You know you take things as they come . . . If the dog is chasing the animals in the wrong direction then you just have to put up with it – if it won't do as it's told. You become resigned to these things.'

On his ambition:

'I'm trying to be a physicist . . . It depends if I'll be good enough to do what I really want to do. I would like, if I can, to do research.'

Nick at 35

'I'm a garrulous person really but I'm seen in all the films as someone who is covering [myself] all the time. It's not in me at all to sit there with tight lips and not say anything. I can keep secrets if it's necessary, sure, but my overriding nature is to want to go out and shout about things.'

> ❛ It would be a disappointment if I didn't achieve very much but I'm not worrying about it . . . I've just got to go out and make it happen. ❜

After I'd done my first degree I did a PhD, which took about two and a half years. Then I went to work for the United Kingdom Atomic Energy Authority doing fusion research. But I found that my standard of living actually went down when I started work, and I couldn't afford what I'd been able to afford as a student. I'd never really worried about making money so it surprised me in a way to discover that I did care about it. The place where I was working had a discouraging atmosphere. Anyway, when I was offered a job in the States I thought it would be a good opportunity to go somewhere where the research environment was a bit more vigorous.

I came to America when I was 24, and when I first arrived the main concerns were about how to survive. It wasn't even clear at first that the job I was coming to really existed. And it's very difficult being plonked down thousands of miles from where you come from – you have no safety net of family to help you through.

At that point I was at the University of Wisconsin, working on high-temperature nuclear fusion, and my overriding concern in life was to keep everything together. Basically I was having a hell of a time. Quite soon after I arrived in Madison we all got lay-off notices, and I remember us all sitting round in the department wondering whether it was for real. I think in the end it was probably a ploy to get more funding for our department, but it did come very close to being the real thing and it wasn't too funny. It was a difficult year for the whole nuclear fusion programme. Every year the research and development budget was being cut back.

The big problem, having come all this way to America for me to do the job that I wanted to do, was how to pay next month's rent. Where to go from here? How to keep going? The pioneer spirit was called for. It was like dodging raindrops to keep the whole thing going.

Nick at 28, on the influence of his rural childhood:
'I was the only child of my age in my village but I managed to spend my time talking to adults who were around. If one is wandering down a country

lane there is an awful lot to look at in the world around you. I remember looking at various natural phenomena and being intrigued to try and understand what made them tick . . . I think that if I'd been in a city I probably would have had more interaction with people and might have developed more skills in dealing with other kids.'

On his choice of research area:
'I picked it [nuclear fusion] because I thought it really was something that could be useful to people, hopefully, eventually.'

On leaving England:
'I'd gone through a wonderful educational system . . . Oxford was a fantastic experience socially and it was a great place to try and develop emotionally. And the academic standards there are superb . . . Having trained in a very academic fashion there, I then went out to try and do something with all that training and found that society just wasn't terribly interested in what I was trying to do.'

On life in America:
'It's an exciting place to be. There's a lot going on in terms of research and other things . . . I think there are more opportunities . . . The place is less hidebound, it's less bureaucratically tied down, so it's much easier to go out and get things done than in England.'

Nick during the filming of *28 Up*.

On having children:
'The big issue for us at the moment is how we're going to have kids and run two careers. We don't want to miss out on the chance of having a significant career and we don't want to miss out on the chance to have kids and to be involved in them.'

Nick at 35:
'I looked forward to it [going to America] but always with apprehension. I'm always apprehensive about how and what I do next. I'm a bit of a pessimist. I didn't really want to go . . . I just felt that I must do it because it was such a great opportunity . . . that if I didn't do it I would miss the tide.'

I am in a building called Babcock Hall at the University of Wisconsin, Madison, administering an exam to my class of undergraduates. Exams are tough on everyone, because we all want to believe the students have learnt more than they have. We are near the Stock Pavilion and there is a distinct cow smell in this section of campus, which reminds me of home. After an hour here we will try to get the exam graded tonight, which will make it a long evening. So this is the mundane side of being a professor – grading exams all night!

This is certainly the sort of job I always wanted. Most of my time is spent doing research. Research is exciting, but it involves a lot of mundane work too. The goal of research is to make a major contribution in some field. Most researchers hope to discover something amazing, even when all the evidence suggests that they are not likely to if they haven't yet. I think I have done some important work – whether other people agree largely remains to be seen. The early indications are good, and I can always try to do better in future.

I work in electrical engineering. I do numerical modelling (I use a computer to calculate the behaviour) of all sorts of electrical and physical systems. The main example I have worked on recently is solving the Boltzmann equation for a plasma (which means finding out how much gas is where and going how fast in a very hot gas). This sort of calculation has a lot of practical applications, and I was able to find a very effective way of doing the calculation which I think should have all sorts of uses. (It consisted of a fast and simple numerical method of evaluating a 'propagator' for the Boltzmann equation. One of the main products of research is articles in journals, so here goes: it was described in *Physical Review Letters*, 63, (1989), page 2361, and is totally fascinating.)

Nobody does this sort of thing for money. My colleagues all grumble that they could do much better elsewhere; I don't know if it's true! Before that I had been concentrating on fusion, which I chose as a topic because I thought it offered tremendous benefits for the future. It became clear that fusion was not going to be supported very well politically, so I have been working in other areas as well.

I have been married since I was at Oxford, and we have a little boy. He is wonderful – and full of energy. He runs around exploring wherever he is, and he keeps us constantly busy. It has been hard to find time to write this!

Over the last 28 years there have been a few times when I could have made a choice to change the direction of my life. I am not sure I know how to, though. Trying to do scientific research in England made things terribly difficult. For some reason science is taken for granted in Britain. That is a mistake because British science is being hurt and that will have serious consequences.

This programme has not affected me much as far as I can tell, except for some of the opinions people (on TV, not normal people) have had about it. It is amazing that people who think of themselves as intelligent will make judgements about the personalities involved, based on the ten minutes they have seen. It is a unique documentary in that the sorts of questions we have been asked expose us in a way I have never seen anyone else have to deal with. One person seemed disillusioned; I expected the audience to be sympathetic, and probably most people were, but not the TV commentators.

In seven years time it would be wonderful, but probably not possible, to be better known for doing research than for having been in this documentary!

Nick during the filming of *35 Up*.

NEIL

' . . . if I can't be an astronaut, I think I'll be a coach driver . . . I'm going to take people to the country and sometimes take them to the seaside and I'll have a big loudspeaker in the motor coach and tell them whereabouts we are and what we're going to do and what the name of the road is and all about that. **,**

When I was seven we lived in a semi-detached in Woolton, a Liverpool suburb. We'd left our first house when I was two, so the one in Woolton was the first house I really became familiar with. I knew all the nooks and crannies both in the house and the garden. There was a kind of den at the bottom of the garden. It was a great place because it was covered by trees and you could go in there and hide away from everybody else. At the back of the garden there was wire netting through to the next garden, and in that house lived a pal of mine. I'd go into the den and we'd chat to each other through the fence and nobody would be any the wiser. I'm told that when I first moved there I thought I had an invisible friend, and I can vaguely recall that.

I have a younger brother and we got on very well, even though I sometimes used to beat him up. I would meticulously set out these race tracks for cars and it would take me ages to set them up. Then he would just come along and charge into it and the whole thing would go all over the place. So I'd thump him, he'd go whining to my parents and I'd get sent to bed without my supper. That used to happen time and time again, so it's surprising I didn't get to hate him. We still get on very well, and going to his wedding was one of the most memorable experiences in my life.

My parents are both teachers, and that meant I normally got my homework done. Sometimes the kids at school were a bit jealous because they thought I was getting extra tuition, which wasn't the case. I was happy at school – I can't remember doing a lot of work. Peter and I were genuinely friends. I used to play games where you just went off by yourself in the school yard and imagined something happening, like America attacking Russia or something like that. You'd be an important character in the story and you'd rendezvous with your mates at the end of it and compare notes. It sounds really daft but we quite enjoyed those games. And if you were a bit of a loner it was a good way of being occupied. You could be away from the crowd without actually feeling guilty. The other lads used to play Cowboys and Indians, and put flags in the flower beds and things like that.

I was pretty happy at home although I always wanted a pet. My father wouldn't have a dog because he said it was too much to worry about. I used to envy children who had dogs and cats and goldfish. When we went on holidays in the Yorkshire Dales the farmer would always have dogs, and we used to love watching the dogs round up the sheep. We perhaps had more admiration for working dogs than pets.

We'd go to Yorkshire two or three times a year, and stay in a very isolated cottage which belonged to a distant relative. We'd go off on walks and I think this is where my love of wild countryside comes from. In fact the landscape was similar to the one here in Shetland – very little in the way of trees and habitation. I used to read a lot. On the last few occasions we went there I took a big pile of books and just sat by the stream near the cottage.

I remember being taken to the Lake District for the first time and being genuinely struck by how beautiful it was. It was autumn, the leaves were changing and they were all falling into the lake. I used to like wandering amongst the gorse bushes when they were flowering. I can always remember feeling a kind of energy in things around me.

As for hobbies, my father's very interested in trains and he used to take my brother and I train-spotting. On one particular trip to Chester I started keeping a train-spotting diary. I remember writing down all the names of the engines and so on. I would have been about eight then. Even now, I still get a thrill from travelling on a train, particularly if it's somewhere I haven't been before, although I no longer have that childhood enthusiasm, I get angry if there aren't any seats, and irritated by the loudspeakers not only telling you the place you're coming to, but the place you're leaving.

My father used to organise school trips, usually just to Belgium or somewhere quite close. I think the first year I went was when I was seven, and I remember the excitement. We had to catch the night train from Liverpool, so we went to bed at seven o'clock and I was tossing and turning. It was like Christmas Eve, I just couldn't sleep. On one occasion – perhaps it was the next time – I couldn't sleep on the night train. So the guard took me into his compartment and told me the names of all the stations, and for somebody who loved trains this was just so wonderful. Even then I loved the Continent and the different way of life, being in a strange place, different smells, different road signs. It was great.

Neil at 7, on university:
'Well, I don't think I need to go to university because I'm not going to be a teacher.'

On fighting:
'We don't do much fighting in school because we think it's horrible and it hurts.'

On life in a town versus the country:
'. . . in the winter if you lived in the country it would be just all wet and there wouldn't be anything for miles around, and you'd get soaked if you tried to go out and there's no shelter anywhere except in your own house. But in the town you can go out on wet, wintery days, 'cos you can always find somewhere to shelter.'

On coloured people:
'. . . ghostly coloured people . . . You think of a purple person with red eyes and yellow feet. And you can't really think of what they really look like.'

On girls:
'I hate her [Caroline]. She's always getting bad-tempered and cross with me . . . she's always saying, "Neil, move your desk forward!"'

On marriage:
'When I get married I don't want to have any children because they're always doing naughty things and making the whole house untidy.'

Neil's father:

'Neil was always fascinated by the idea of travel and by maps of every kind. Even as a youngster of seven or eight, when we had family holidays in the Lake District, he enjoyed planning the journey and our daily excursions. Using an Ordnance Survey map, and one of our much-thumbed copies of "Wainwright", he would take great delight in guiding our walks and climbs on the fells – and did it very well. Later, he spent much of his pocket money on maps, many of which are still in his desk drawer.

'He and his younger brother loved nothing better than to accompany me on regular Saturday trips to various football matches up and down the country. Neil always followed the route on a map and timed the train between stations. In his teens this hobby gave him even greater pleasure. He used to buy excursion tickets so that he could explore new areas of the rail network, and was often away from home all day, from dawn to dusk.

'The boys always came with us on organised school holidays abroad and soon Neil was keen to use his "Rover" tickets in Europe too. So by the time he left home for university at 18, he was a confident and seasoned traveller.'

Neil with his dad, 1964.

Neil at 35:

'[In a way it was an] over-imaginative . . . over-sensational [childhood] . . . Perhaps I had so much stimulation that after that it was like being on a trip – you know, a junkie's trip – and then everything suddenly came back to reality, very horrible reality.'

AT 14

❛ I think it is a very good idea to have competition otherwise you might start to relax really and not sort of try hard enough. ❜

At school I'd been encouraged by the teachers to feel I was bright and I was contributing a lot to the class. But when I got to secondary school it was toughness and worldliness that were important to the other pupils and whatever I had to offer was not valued. My parents couldn't really identify with the kind of rough children I was dealing with. Being teachers

Neil at 14.

themselves, they had set ideas about how these problems should be dealt with. I honestly think they did their best but they just weren't able to back me up.

By 14 I'd recovered somewhat from the emotional traumas of the first two years in the school. Peter was still a pal but not quite so much of a close pal by that time. I was beginning to be more accepted by the people around me but it was still a battle. In a way, appearing on the programme was a bit of a setback because I was portrayed – whether deliberately or not – as being a nice respectable 14-year-old. And, of course, to the other pupils, it wasn't right to be respectable at the school I was at. I mean, typically, I should have been filmed in a gang fight or going off to an X film or something like that. In fact, I was shown sitting at a nice table in my parents' home talking about doing schoolwork, and that did not fit my cronies' image of the typical 14-year-old. They didn't like to think I was representing them – that was the problem.

I remember saying at 14 that I didn't think I was mature enough to have a girlfriend and I made that as a very serious comment. I felt it was a perceptive view of my situation. I wasn't moving in the same circles as my mates, I was still really into Enid Blyton and a sort of fantasy world.

As for becoming aware of social class, the only incident I can remember is staying in a holiday home in Scotland when I was about 14, and finding that some of the people staying there were going skiing afterwards. I suddenly realised that our family, whatever we did, were never going to go skiing. This was something that was actually not open to everybody.

The first year my parents let me go on my own on the railway was 1969. I only went as far as somewhere like Crewe – it was a big day out. I just felt very free and very grown-up, buying my own ticket. The next year, when I was about 13, I went to stay with my aunt in Oxford and when I got there I made a few excursions out to the countryside. After that I began to go much further afield. In 1971 I travelled up to Scotland and various other places. That was when I first came to Scotland. It went into my soul – it had a very deep effect.

Neil at 14, on his school:
'And then I moved up to the comprehensive school. I found it much bigger of course, and I found it hard to settle into at first . . . You get to know different types of people. People with different sorts of brains, you know. From the very clever people to the people who haven't got much sense at all really . . .'

'In Set One it's very, very hard to keep up with the leaders. I never have time to relax at all.'

On girls:
'Perhaps I'm not mature enough yet to be interested.'

On coloured people:
'Well, personally, I've got nothing against coloured people. I think they're the same as everybody else. But it seems that there is a lot of argument about them . . . as any foreigners really . . . that are taking up people's jobs in England . . .'

On religion:
'Yes, I'd say I believed in God . . . I go to church with my parents on Sunday.'

On being rich:
'If you're healthy and have good friends you can get on perfectly well . . . But everybody would like to be rich.'

On politics:
'I don't think I would have voted at all [in the last general election] because I don't know enough about it, really.'

On travel:
'I used to go . . . with my father . . . he used to take school parties abroad . . . I enjoyed Switzerland mostly. I think it's a very beautiful country. I also enjoyed Austria but not to such a great extent. Those are my favourite two countries. I've been to France and Belgium and Holland as well but I didn't find them as interesting.'

Neil on holiday in Yorkshire.

Neil at 35:
'I chose to go to the comprehensive because most of the people I knew were going there . . . the grammar school was the sort of very posh place . . . My parents actually tried to get me to go to the grammar school and I resisted them . . . Perhaps I don't regret it because I saw a side of life that I might have been sheltered from. I don't regret experiences. There's no experience I've had that I regret having.'

❛ I don't think I ever had any stability, to be quite honest. I can't think of any time in my life when I did . . . I think I've been kicking in mid-air all my life. ❜

I left university because I was very unhappy. I'd set my sights on Oxford and I didn't get in. To me, anywhere else was second-best. It wouldn't have mattered where it was. I went to Aberdeen University and – having travelled most of the summer, done very exciting things and met all kinds of people – I then found myself with a group of people who'd barely left school. Unfortunately the hall of residence was very strong Scottish nationalist and English people just weren't accepted. I felt that even some of the senior staff didn't seem to be interested in this kind of social problem. The only people who were willing to speak to me were Christians who I felt were patronising me.

My main interest at that time, and earlier, was literature. I've always loved reading and drama. At first I wrote poems, then I wrote my first novel at 16. I'd written about four novels by the time I was 21 and after that I just gave it up, apart from more poetry, various other articles and non-fiction books.

At 21 I was in London, living in a squat and working on a building site. I didn't enjoy the work on the building site but it was a worthwhile experience. I left the job after the programme came out and I didn't stay in London long – I was soon back in Scotland. I kept slightly in contact with my brother, but my relationship with the rest of the family was virtually non-existent.

Neil at 21.

Neil at 21, on university:

'I only took university seriously for a couple of months . . . Maybe I went to the wrong university or maybe the university life didn't suit me. Either way I felt a great need to get out of the system.'

'I did make an application to Oxford but I didn't get in. That's in the past now. I don't know whether I would have been any happier at Oxford. It had always been a dream to get into Oxford, I think because people had encouraged me and because I knew famous people had been to Oxford . . . but . . . well, they were only dreams which I had when I was at school. I will have to just get over the fact that I didn't get into Oxford . . . I was very, very bitter at the time – maybe I still am – but I try to get over it.'

On squatting:

'I wouldn't squat in a place which I knew to be owned by somebody else. I wouldn't because I know if I had a place of my own and found somebody squatting in it I would be disgusted. But this place was empty and I was simply offered a place to live and was very grateful for it. I think in questions of squatting a bit of humanity is more important than vain rules about who can live where.'

'I've got my own room, I can cook whenever I like. I haven't got a landlady to tell me what time to come in. I've got my own front door key. To tell you the truth, it's a lot better than a lot of accommodation I've had over the last 18 months or so . . . It could be a bit warmer . . . but it's perfectly satisfactory for the time being.'

On his parents:

'I don't think I was really taught any sort of policy of living at all by my parents . . . I was left to fend for myself in a world which they seemed completely oblivious of . . .'

'. . . they've often said to me that they had seen me even from when I was very young in a certain type of career, and possibly they never even thought that anything else was vaguely possible. They probably imagined I would be maybe a university lecturer or a bank manager or something like that . . . I wonder how many parents really think of their children as individual human beings.'

'I'm capable of getting on with my parents perfectly well *if* they are willing to let me live as another adult in their house and appreciate that I am living my own way of life and that I am living there because I cannot think of anything else to do with myself.'

'We have, in fact, managed to discuss a lot of personal things which I felt at one time I would never be able to discuss.'

On religion:

'. . . they [my parents] made me believe in God for a start . . . they made it absolutely certain that if one was to survive in the world one would have to believe in God.'

On himself at 7:
'I find it hard to believe I was ever like that but there's the evidence . . . I wonder what it was inside me that made me like that . . . Probably when I was seven I lived in a wonderful world where everything was a warm sensation and I could be happy one minute and I could be miserable the next minute. I didn't have to plan for the future, I didn't have to worry about having friends. Everything was so mapped out for me.'

On himself:
'I think maybe . . . I didn't have enough obstacles to get over, to toughen myself up against. I was unprepared for things as they were but, looking back, even now, I couldn't think what might have been done. And I certainly wouldn't start writing educational theories about this because I know how personal a thing it is.'

On the situation he hoped to be in at 28:
'In a job, from which I was getting satisfaction. Married, probably with children, with a good salary – enough to, as I said before, to be able to live fairly comfortably. And with friends whom I could contact when I wanted to.'

On his ambition:
'I would like to be somebody in a position of some importance . . . But I don't think, in actual fact, I would be the right sort of person to carry responsibility. I always thought, well, I would love to be . . . in politics or something . . . But I suppose I'd probably find that just as tedious as all the other jobs I've done . . .'

On what he wanted out of life:
'Simply to be able to wake up in the morning and feel that this day was worthwhile . . . which I don't do at the moment.'

Neil at 35:
'I think it was very important to see what I couldn't do, to see people who could do it perfectly well, but nevertheless weren't altogether happy. I think it gave me a sense of life – what some people have to do all the time . . . I did a bit more labouring after that in Scotland but it made me realise I could never do it for the rest of my life.'

❛ Well, I'm still known as an eccentric, as I have been since the age of 16 or so. But I don't mind. I think that is, in some ways, acceptable. **❜**

After *21 Up* I worked on another project in Aberdeen for the summer and I think I've spent most of the time since then in and out of Scotland. It's the people and the countryside that have kept me here – all good things always go together. The Scottish people are proud of their countryside, and proud of the fact that they spend a little bit more time coming to judgements than people do in other countries sometimes. That doesn't suit everyone, but you don't have to be instantaneous in Scotland.

When *28 Up* was made, I'd spent the summer on a farm in North Wales and I'd just arrived in the Western Highlands of Scotland. In Wales I was living in a caravan and moved to a farmhouse until the end of August. I'd done a bit of work in the theatre at Aberdeen over the previous few years and the last job I'd had was cooking in a youth hostel. At 28 I was living on social security and eating a bit better. In Aberdeen there had been times when I really was short of food.

Neil at 28, on his life:
'The last three years I've been unemployed but travelling quite a bit, mostly in Britain . . . I live off money from social security which does me for my rent and my food . . . If the state didn't give us any money it would point you towards crime, and I'm glad I don't have to steal to keep myself alive. . . . If the money runs out . . . I simply have to find the warmest shed I can find.'

On his education:
'I think unfortunately I grew up against a background of . . . people of pretty average intelligence . . . I know I went to university expecting to be something of a genius in fact, and this wasn't the case at all.'

'No formal education can prepare anybody for life. Only life can prepare you for what comes.'

On himself at 21:

'I think I was venomous and . . . had I been in an easier situation myself . . . I would have been perhaps a little kinder. I had to take out my anger on somebody and I think it came out on my parents . . . perhaps unconsciously a lot of what I said was what I did feel underneath. But I don't want the scar to remain.'

On himself at 7:

'I know at seven years old I was fascinated by everything around me . . . the colours of things that were funny, the sounds that people made . . . I had, if you like, idiosyncratic views about things that other people hadn't even thought about.'

On himself:

'I don't think I've been typical of the environment in which I lived. I might still have been unemployed but what my background has given me is a sense of just being part of a very impersonal society.'

On suburban life:

'The suburbs force this kind of feeling upon somebody. The most you can hope to achieve is to have the right to climb into a suburban train five or ten times a week and just about stagger back for the weekend. The least is just unemployment.'

'The cheap satisfaction of so many things . . . the aimlessness . . . Nobody seems to know where they, or anybody else, is going and nobody seems to worry. You know, you finish the week, you come home, you plug into the TV set, and the weekend. And then you manage to get back to work on Monday and it seems to me that this is just a slow pass to total brain-washing. And if you have a brain-washed society then you're heading towards doom . . .'

'I'm not claiming that I feel as though I'm in some sort of Nirvana, but I'm claiming that if I was living in a bedsit in suburbia I'd be so miserable I'd feel like cutting my throat . . .'

On religion:

'. . . in the Old Testament God is very unpredictable. And that's, I think, how I see him in my life, sometimes very benevolent, sometimes seemingly needlessly unkind.'

Neil during the filming of 28 Up.

On having children:

'I always told myself that I would never have children . . . because children inherit something from their parents. And even if my wife were the most high-spirited and ordinary and normal of people, the child would still stand a very fair chance of being not totally full of happiness because of what he or she will have inherited from me.'

On his health problems:

'I have always had a nervous complaint. I've had it since I was 16. It was responsible for my leaving university and for some of my difficulties with work.'

'I've occasionally had to see doctors, yes. I haven't had any treatment . . . I've had a lot of advice. But you know the best medicine is kind words and it usually comes from somebody who has nothing to do with the medical profession. Which isn't to say that the doctors can't be very helpful. But really the thing a sick person wants is to be away from doctors as soon as possible.'

On his parents:

'We made up quite well after the bad times we went through when I was in my early twenties . . . I think suddenly it perhaps almost mutually dawned upon us that we were all making mistakes and also that some of the things we did couldn't be helped. And I think now that perhaps the greatest thing we have achieved is we know when to say nothing and . . . we know when to be tolerant of each other . . . and that's really tremendous. What I'd like most of all would be to be able to do something for my parents when they're older, to be there . . .'

On his future:

'. . . it seemed to me for a long time that getting a reliable job and a nice place to live would be the solution. Well, I haven't succeeded . . . I can't see any immediate future at all. But here I am . . . I've still got clothes on my back, not particularly nice clothes, but I've got them. I have a place to go to, I have some prospects of work, I'm still applying for jobs, I haven't given up.'

'I'm a lot happier now than I was seven years ago. I'm more content. I don't have such dreadful yearnings. I don't feel so hopelessly as if everything is against me . . . I'm just somebody with my own particular difficulties, and my own particular obstacles to surmount . . .'

Writing in a Wilderness by Neil

Each year, at our local pantomime, the frog, or the Beast, or whatever it is, usually turns into a handsome Prince. Or, if he or she is unlucky, the Prince or the other hero or heroine of the show turns into a gorilla – for a while, anyway. Of course, that's not me there, on the stage. In my life, and in the lives of 13 other (young) people of exactly my age, it happens only once every seven years. When it does happen, though, it's for real.

Thirty-five: what does it mean to me? Or to you, rather? To *you* it probably means: you're never going to be a film-actress, to play test cricket at the Oval or the piano at the Royal Festival Hall; experience cramp after tennis or exhilaration after football again, or nausea after eating a piece of cheese which you didn't like to refuse because the lady who gave it to you was an ex-acquaintance of your parents. It could, indeed, mean going back to meat after years of vegetarianism. It could signify being able to put up with the noise of the launderette (i.e. not needing to go for a walk while the spin-dryer is on); yearning for the past (something which you might have been doing since you were 25, in fact), and the holidays in Tenerife (if you're lucky enough to get them) are starting to be a bore: the kids are asking you more and more questions; you think about the notion of religion, then reject it, for the tenth time. And one remembers Robert Lowell's emphatic complaint, made at a slightly later stage in his development:

'How we wish we were friends with half our friends!'

At the age of 35 the 'I' of Dante's *Divine Comedy* claims to have lost the narrow way, only to regain it later through love, while the heroes of most novels, even those of unknown secondary school teachers of English who write in their spare time, always 'come good' at 35.

Thirty-five is the 'sexy' age, *n'est-ce pas?* At 35 all men are braw, hunky – and smoke cigars, don't they? And all women wear sunglasses pulled back over their long, drawn-out (often straw-coloured), flowing locks, promenade everywhere in home-made dresses of ankle-length, sip Bacardi or Pimms out of crystal glasses and sit glued to Kylie and the rest. Actually – to change the subject a little – I've met Suzy of *Seven* + 7 + 7 . . . since the last programme and she isn't like that. True, their car – was it a Citroën? – is either French or Italian, but it was about 15 years old – then – and the paint is surely peeling by now. Neither are the other three – Jackie, Lynn and Sue –

Neil at 35.

like that. Come on, you must have seen the programmes more often than I have. They would be most offended to be considered so. I wonder if 45 will be – having said all this – even sexier? And will Michael Apted know?

And 35 for me? It will mean – unless the *35 Up* programme earns me a significant promotion – continuing to live in the world of hopeless failure. It is an exile I am living in Shetland which, although very pleasant in its own way, keeps me apart from that life I really want to inhabit and inter-react with. True, I help to run – to organise – a small amateur drama group which has been moderately successful and which we (the other members of the cast and I) would like to develop further (perhaps to take on tour); and shouldn't I be satisfied with all this? I have a roof over my head, too – I am on the local hall committee, and I attend a village church.

Neil at 35 in Shetland.

It remains to be asked: why am I here? Largely because of Thatcher politics. Not because of a direct, sinister influence trying to bear me down (although there have been times when I have suspected even that), but because of the lazy, almost incompetent attitudes of *laissez-faire* which are so prevalent in this country at the moment; attitudes which attach no value to artistic creation and leave the creative core of society – and are artists and writers not its core – not to rot in good earth, where it would produce good fruit, but on hideous display in poor-quality glass cages, badly aired, even if ventilated and serviced (somewhat grudgingly) by the Department of Health and Social Security. The earth is barren. Nothing will grow in it. Only Mrs Thatcher can still cultivate it, and she has planted here and there her own brand of artificially fertilised wheat which (when it does spring up) is proud for a day, and then is shorn by that great combine harvester called political economy, leaving an infertile and unusable scrubland behind it on almost every occasion.

Finally, how do I spend my time? Well, I write an hour or two in the morning, perhaps – then read for a while. Then there's usually some business to be done in the local shop, or in the post office, or around my washing-line; followed, sometimes, by a visit to friends. Or, if I can't think of any friends to visit, I'll just take a walk up on some nearby headland, or along to the pier, or the lighthouse, or somewhere on the shore. Anywhere, just so long as it passes a few minutes, or maybe an hour or so. There's usually a trip to Lerwick on Thursdays. Or I can come indoors, masturbate, and cook an egg or a couple of beefburgers. In the summer, if the weather's fine, there's a plot of land I have that I can go out and dig in for a few moments.

On sunny days it's not hard to imagine Viking longships sailing up the voe, laden with their brigades of warriors who will plunder here first, then settle down quietly to inhabit surrounding territory.

Now, however, there are no more longships; Tor and Odin are just driving combine harvesters – unusually big ones at that. Some of the apple-cores don't even get into cages, either – they are just thrown in the wake of the gods. Whose soil are they going to plough up next?

Neil surrounded by his books.

PETER

❝ . . . if I can't be an astronaut, I think I'll be a sergeant in the police force, like my dad is. ❞

I grew up in Liverpool. My father is Welsh, he was in the police force, and my mother was a housewife. When I was seven we were living in Woolton, a South Liverpool suburb, and I was attending Woolton County Primary School. I had a brother, who was two years younger than me, and a newly arrived sister. I also had relatives in Liverpool and North Wales. My family knew Neil's family through the local church and I'd known Neil since we were five.

Peter at 7, on girls:
'. . . when we catch them we kiss them. And when it's "Catch a boy, kiss a boy", when the girls catch us they kiss us.'

'Well, once Caroline said that she loved me. And I'm going to marry her when I grow up.'

On fighting:
'We play Richard the Lionheart and William Tell.'

On university:
'I don't think you ought to go to university if you want to be an astronaut.'

Peter (*second from right*) with his mother, younger brother and baby sister.

‘ . . . [competition] is a good thing. Probably if there was no one to compete with you, you wouldn't be trying as hard. **‚**·

Having jumped the final year of primary school, I went to Gateacre Comprehensive at ten. I consequently lost touch with many friends from junior school but not with Neil, who had made a similar leap. My family were still living in Woolton.

Peter at 14, on money:
'I usually get 5 to 6 bob a week . . . I save some, spend some.'

'I wouldn't mind [being rich].'

On strikes:
'It's a big problem and causes quite a lot of discussion. I think the workers do tend to take a few liberties as regards strikes.'

On politics:
'I think they [the political parties] are all as bad as each other really.'

On travel:
'I've never been abroad. Travel doesn't really interest me much. I'm happy where I am.'

On newspapers:
'We get the *Daily Mail* and the *Echo* . . . [I only read] the back page . . . for the sport.'

On religion:
'I wouldn't say I'm deeply religious, but I do believe in God.'

On wanting to be an astronaut when he was 7:
'Well, I've changed my mind completely of course. I mean, it was just the imagination a seven-year-old has.'

Peter at 14.

On what he wanted out of life:
'I just want to get on well if possible with other people . . . Have enough
to live comfortably.'

Peter at 35:
'I was as withdrawn as most 14-year-old boys, perhaps more so as a
result of being a year younger than my classmates.'

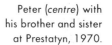

Peter (*centre*) with
his brother and sister
at Prestatyn, 1970.

6 Perhaps we haven't got full democracy – in
fact we probably haven't – but it's a pretty
good system. 9

This is where Granada lost their synchronisation, never since recovered – I
was 20! I was in my final year reading History at London University, sharing a
flat in North London with three lads I'd met at the hostel I'd initially been in:
one is still a close friend. I won a bet with Michael Apted over the outcome of
the European Cup quarter-final. I had no career plans.

Peter at 21, on leaving Liverpool:
'It was obviously a big step. It was exciting really. Well, that sounds corny, but
it was . . . It was pouring down with rain and I had the traditional send-off
from Lime Street. My mum and dad were there. A couple of mates turned up
at the last minute from the school to see me off.'

On his life as a student:
'Well, this is my final year, so I'm not in college that much – I don't have to
be . . .'

'. . . once I get myself going I can work solid, yes. But it's the motive that's
very hard to acquire when you're at the flat. It's hard to look ahead to next
June and think of those exams. I daresay I'll do it and get the average-type
degree. I'm not worried.'

'. . . it can be [a problem motivating myself]. I look back on a day and think, hell, what a waste of time. Although I might have enjoyed it at the time.'

On marriage:
'It doesn't appeal to me at all at the moment. I'm just gone 20. I haven't been abroad yet. There's no way I'm going to get settled down.'

On his future:
'Obviously I've got to get a job. I don't want to laze around on the dole for months and months, I mean, you'd go mad. But I just can't see what I will be doing in nine months or ten months time . . . It certainly doesn't depress me. Perhaps it does excite me in a way . . . Something will turn up . . . but obviously you've got to think realistically about doing something. I mean, I might be living in cloud cuckoo land. My mum and dad might say, "Now, son, that's not life. You'll not get a job you like." I'd like to think I could.'

On his fears for the future:
'. . . the idea . . . of getting into a job, and sort of getting stuck in it . . . Without knowing why you're doing it . . . this is the time to think about something like that, to make sure it doesn't happen.'

On what he wanted out of life:
'The satisfaction of knowing that I've left some sort of imprint, rather than just lived out my life . . . then again, it's just a drop in the ocean, I suppose. I mean, who's going to remember you in a hundred years time? But I would like to think I'm doing something . . . positive.'

Peter at 35:
'I suppose we were typical male students, i.e. spotty, pretentious, wearing appalling clothes. But it was a very happy time and educational in the broadest sense.'

Peter at 21.

'I don't want to drag you into party politics, you know, but basically it's the most incompetent uncaring bloody shower we've ever had. '

AT 28

When they made *28 Up* I'd been teaching for five years in a large mixed comprehensive outside Leicester. Why Leicester? It was where the job came up. I was married and we were living in our own terrace house in *Guardian*-reader-land. The filming took place at a point where I'd had enough of working in an 'exam factory' – I left that December. I could never settle in the Midlands but Liverpool seems to have a pull on its natives that nowhere else does.

Peter at 28, on the education system:
'Teachers are undervalued and under-rated. The whole . . . system is beginning to crumble. People outside of it don't realise it but it is. And it's very disillusioning. You don't feel you're getting anywhere. And, of course, the money as well, which whatever the papers tell you, is abysmal.'

Peter during the filming of *28 Up*.

On himself:
'The facts were that I'm not a particularly intelligent person – just reasonably, I suppose. I'm not a genius. I just went to college on three reasonable A-levels and . . . did the bare minimum – turned up to lectures, wrote a few essays. You get a degree for it . . .'

'If I've got things to do I'd sooner make a cup of tea first and read the paper.'

On himself at 7:
'. . . after that, you know, your barriers begin to go up and you learn how to fend off things . . . and obviously when you're seven you don't think about it, you just come out with it. Yeah, so to a point, you reflect [the man] . . .'

On having children:
'. . . we've both got things we still prefer to be doing, you know. You have children and that immediately limits you. I don't want to be limited yet.'

On how he would educate his own children:
'. . . teach them more relevant things. Get them to think for themselves, which schools don't do enough.'

'. . . private schools help to keep the old class system going. They're part of it, they perpetuate it. So I'm certainly not going to be involved in that.'

On equality of opportunity:
'Well, other people have got it made for them still, haven't they? They've got it all lined up.'

On his best moment:
'Tommy Smith scoring the second goal in Rome . . . That was the European Cup Final, 1977 . . . nothing else compares with it really.'

Peter at 35:
'I was very "right on" by this time – a member of the Labour Party and CND. The *Sun* and *Daily Mail* loved me.'

I've been asked to describe the world through the eyes of a 35-year-old. The thing is, I can't do that. At the time of writing, I am actually only 33. Pedantic, perhaps, and maybe the protest of a man who realises that he will not now play for Liverpool, but true, nevertheless. There is a gap between the image and the truth but then, that's always been the case. Granada have been getting our ages wrong for a long time now. When they filmed *21 Up*, I was 20. For *28 Up*, read 27, and now this. Where will it end? Will we have *Pensioners Up* while we're still in our forties? In itself, that's not really serious, of course, but it does say something to me about Granada and their children, which is important to understand.

Let me put my cards on the table before I go any further. I regret having appeared on the programmes and I will not be seen in *35 Up* or whatever it's going to be called. I felt the same the last time and the time before that but, I'm ashamed to say, the money was persuasive. It won't be this time because I have had enough of my life being used for small screen entertainment. Entertainment: remember that. It's what this is all about. It's not about art or sociology, but entertainment. Granada are in the business of entertainment and, these days, it's big business. *Seven Up* and its sequels were created primarily to make Granada successful in that business. It might be stating the obvious to say so, as we watch the quality now being squeezed out of British television by the money, but *35 Up*, just like the others, will keep to a tried and tested format. Nothing will be left to chance. No challenging statements will be made or questions posed about our country today. The image will be carefully packaged and presented, just like in any other big business. The casualty, as ever, will be the truth and the gap between seems to grow ever wider. This could be dismissed as standard left-wing paranoia of the media and it's fair to say that I have a concern about the direction in which they're headed in the nineties. However, my own experience of the nature of television and the press reinforces my every suspicion.

Peter at 33.

I'm not being vain when I say that I don't think that Granada have ever known quite how to pigeon-hole me. They will say, of course, that they didn't set out to pigeon-hole anyone, but how would *Seven Up* otherwise have got off the ground? An investigation into a pervasive class system with children drawn at random from any class? It doesn't hold water. Quite obviously, we were categorised from the very start. That didn't matter so much when we were seven. Back in 1964, the demarcations and barriers were still clearly marked anyway, as yet undisturbed by the tremors of that decade. In any case, seven-year-olds can get by on charm alone. The children in that first programme were mainly cast as toffs or tykes: the spoilt brats of the ruling class, whom you booed, and the loveable kids from the backstreets, who were the salt of the earth. You could see the same social structure in any of the Ealing comedies and, to be fair, that was still very much the England in which we lived. Then there were Neil and myself.

I think, at that stage, that we were the token middle classes. Again, that was possibly a fair representation for the early sixties but Granada were short-sighted. Nobody had perceived the fundamental shifts in the class system which were becoming noticeable even then. Money was actually filtering down to the traditional working class and the effect was to alter radically the composition of our society as portrayed in *Seven Up*. By the end of the decade, there was the basis of almost a new class, made up of children of working-class parents, but who couldn't be called working class any longer. They'd had the benefits of the Welfare State in its prime, had gone to well-funded comprehensive schools, maybe on to college and then into teaching, social work or white-collar jobs, where good prospects awaited them. More than Neil, more than anyone else in *Seven Up*, I embodied all this. Granada, though, missed it. Instead, I am remembered as the little boy who wanted to be an astronaut. How cute. How entertaining.

As seven turned to 14 and so on, the programmes could no longer get by on the cuteness of the participants. Have you ever seen a cute 14-year-old? Has there ever been a 14-year-old with enough to say to fill a television interview? More to the point, the seventies saw the burgeoning of this new class, or sub-class, to which I belonged and yet I remained its only representative among Granada's children. There was still no attempt to examine that on any serious level. The image from *21 Up* that lingered (by design, I suspect) was of two hapless flatmates and myself making our tea; lads away from home, blundering round the kitchen, burning the sausages. Well, fall about! Still the series trundled on. By the time of *28 Up*, it seemed to have lost any sense of direction or purpose.

I had now gone through the system and come out the other side as a teacher in a comprehensive school, married and a home-owner. By now, of course, that system had all but collapsed. The liberalism of the sixties and early seventies had ebbed away with the oil crisis, and Margaret Thatcher had come along to tell us all how wrong we'd been to believe in the 'nanny state' in the first place. That meant that the people of my background and generation felt the squeeze, as the public sector, where so many of us were based, was stripped to the bone. In my case, it resulted in increasing despair over the running-down of the education system and the consequent decrease in opportunities for teachers and children alike. At no point did I feel especially sorry for myself: that woman has caused deeper suffering to many other people. Yet, if you'd have watched *28 Up*, you'd have come away with the impression that I was a bitter and negative person. Given the chance to look beyond that image, Granada just dwelt on clichés, which the newspaper columnists gleefully picked on. I was variously described as the last of the angry young men, a teacher to whom you wouldn't want to entrust your children and basically a miserable sod. Friends reassured me that, as the newspapers in question were toilet-roll substitutes, I must have said the right things. I'd always taken a similar dismissive view of those rags but, believe me, it's different when you're in their firing-line and I was shocked and upset.

There and then, I called a halt to my further involvement in Granada's
overgrown baby.

I agreed to contribute to this book because I saw it as a chance to
articulate, in a way television would never allow me, how I feel about the
series now. It's been important to me to set that down and then break with
the past for ever. *Seven Up* must have seemed like a good idea at the time
and it was probably a worthwhile programme as a one-off. The sequels,
however, have been a classic example of television flogging a winner to death.
Millions may have watched, money was made, but shouldn't there be more to
it than that? The images of myself and of the other Granada children and of
many people, as portrayed by television and the press, have been tailored for
mass consumption: the lowest common denominator. The images have thus
been distorted and simplified to the point where they have become false.
Aren't human beings infinitely more complicated and interesting than that?
Aren't they worth more?

If you should see any of the programmes, please don't think that they're
telling you anything about me. If you want the truth, turn the TV off and
come to Liverpool.

Peter in Liverpool.

SUZY

AT 7

❝ When I leave this school I'm down for Heathfield and Southover Manor, and then maybe I may want to go to a university, but I don't know which one yet. ❞

Suzy at seven.

At seven I was living with my mother, father and nanny in a flat overlooking Hyde Park in London. I was really brought up by Nan. She's 84 now and has been with our family for 50 years, having gone on to look after my eldest half-sister's children when she left me when I was eight. I don't know how to describe her but she was always there for me and most memories of my early childhood include her. I can remember seeing photographs of her when she first came. There's this wonderful picture of her with her grey flannel coat and her grey flannel hat pulled right down. Nan had also looked after my three half-sisters. The eldest, Sally, is 17 years older than me, then Carolyn and Sunny. They were away at boarding school or left home by the time I was seven, so to all intents and purposes, I was an only child. I was at Lady Eden's, a day school in London, when the infamous Mr Apted first found me.

I can remember going to children's parties sometimes, but I don't remember having many friends in London. We had a flat in Sandwich Bay where we used to go for weekends and holidays, and I think I probably had more of a normal social life there. One girl who was also an only child is still one of my greatest friends and a god-mother to my daughter Laura.

Suzy at 7 on her daily routine:
'Well, I go home, I go and see my mother and I have tea and watch TV, then I do my homework and I go and see my father.'

'Last night I didn't go to bed till seven.'

On having children:
'When I get married I'd like to have two children. I want a nanny to look after them.'

Suzy at 35:
'I listen to Ru (my husband) now – there's five of them [in his family] – discussing all the family holidays and the things they all got up to. I didn't have any of that, it was very, very different.'

6 I'd like to do, maybe shorthand typing or something like that. 9

We moved to Scotland when I was nine and I think it was a very traumatic stage of my life. Nan had really been the backbone of my life and suddenly she left and I was packed off to boarding school in Dunkeld, which I hated. It was all so new up there.

The school was about 32 miles away from home but we weren't often allowed home for weekends. My father was semi-retired and working part-time as a stockbroker in London, so my parents weren't always there anyway. My aunt and uncle lived very near and would come and take me out.

I left the school in Dunkeld when I was 11 and went to another boarding school in Sussex, coming back to Scotland for holidays. My father was almost retired by now and spending very little time in the South.

Those school days in England were slightly happier, but I can't honestly say I relished boarding school. I suppose there was the companionship of other children which I wasn't going to get at home. There are a few girls that I am still in close contact with now, and I vaguely know what has happened to the other people in the class. We didn't have any contact with boys; if a boy was seen within a 2-mile radius of the school gates, they almost called the police.

By 14 I was enjoying living in Scotland. I had a pony and loved being there, but I was a loner and I used to spend hours on my own. I was too old for a nanny as such, but I had an endless succession of so-called companions who were employed to amuse or look after me.

I can remember very clearly having to do the programme. I woke up that morning thinking I was either going to run away or I wasn't going to get out of bed, I couldn't decide which. At 14 you're not a child or an adult and I think it is the most awkward time in anybody's life. Looking back at the performances some of us gave at seven, there was a huge change at 14, nobody was the extrovert at 14.

Suzy during the filming of *Seven Plus Seven*.

Suzy at 14, on her life in Scotland:
'There's always something to do here, I'm never bored. I ride, swim, play tennis, ping pong. And I might play croquet, something like that.'

On politics:
'In the last general election I'd have voted Conservative . . . Why? I just don't like Labour. I don't know . . . I mean, I don't really know much about politics. It doesn't interest me so I never really bother.'

On the programme:
'I just think it's ridiculous . . . What's the point of going into people's lives and saying, "Why do you like this and why don't you?" I don't see any point in it.'

Suzy at 35:
'I think at 14 I was beginning to start the phase in my life that I look back on and try to block out. My parents were getting divorced, I was very insecure, very confused and just lived life day to day without looking very much ahead.'

❛ . . . when you're a child you always think how nice it will be to be grown up and independent and things, but there are times when I wish I was three again. ❜

You're very restricted living at boarding school and my parents never gave me a huge amount of freedom, so when I finally moved into a flat with some friends, I nearly let the independence rule me, which is where it could all have gone so wrong.

By 21 I was sharing a flat with the girl I had known so well in Sandwich Bay. We had done a secretarial course together and we both had jobs in London. I was working for a residential Anglo-Belgian Club as an assistant to the Club Secretary. I then worked for an advertising and public relations company, before working for the managing director of a hotel, where I worked up until the time I married Rupert. Sometimes I regret not having made more of a career, but at the crucial time I didn't seem to care.

I had had a few boyfriends by this stage, some more serious than others. There was one relationship at a particularly difficult time which was wonderful, but sadly it would never have worked in the long term. When I was 15, 16, 17, the thought of ever being married and going through what my parents had been through, really terrified me. By 21 I was a bit less frightened of marriage.

Suzy at 21.

Suzy at 21, on herself at 14:
'Well, I didn't want to do it [the programme] when I was 14. I know I was difficult because I was very anti doing it. I was pressurised into doing it by my parents . . . I hated it and vowed I'd never do it now, but here I am.'

On her life since 16:
'I left school when I was 16 and went to Paris, went to secretarial college and got a job . . . I just wasn't interested in school and wanted to get away.'

'I've always been lucky up to a certain point, but everyone has their bad times and I'm only just beginning. I'm only young and I'll probably have a lot worse than I've been through now.'

On the city versus the country:

'At the moment I could never live in the country . . . The country is nice for four days – going for long healthy walks, but I could never live there now.'

On her parents' divorce:

'. . . aged 14, you're at a very vulnerable age and it does cut you up. You know, you get over it. There was no point in them staying together for me because it was worse – I mean the rows . . . And if two people can't live together then there's no point in making yourself, even for the sake of the children.'

On marriage:

'I haven't given it a lot of thought because I'm very, very cynical about it. But then again, you get a certain amount of faith restored in it. I've got friends and their parents are happily married and so it does put faith back into you. But I'm very cynical about it.'

'At the moment I just don't really believe in it . . . I've got no desire to [get married] . . . I think 20's far too young.'

On having children:

'I'm not very children-minded at the moment. I don't know if I ever will be . . . I don't like babies.'

Suzy at 35:

'I suppose those years . . . 17 to 21, were years I look back on now and think, I could have made a hell of a mess of my life . . . I think I was lucky – I don't really know how or why – but somehow somebody must have been on my side and I just didn't get engrossed in a bigger mess than I was heading for.'

Suzy on her wedding day, age 22.

❛ I feel if I was going to have fallen by the wayside, I would have done it by now. I think probably I'm too staid now to do that. But maybe I'm wrong. ❜

AT 28

People sometimes say to me, 'At 21, there you were saying you didn't believe in marriage and yet the next year you were married to Rupert.' In fact, I was only 20 when the *21* programme was filmed, so it was more than two years. We got married in November 1978 and lived in London for a further two and a half years. We then decided that we would like to move out of London and live in the country. Rupert found a job as a solicitor in 1981.

Three very profound things happened to me between the ages of 21 and 28: marriage, my father's death and having children. Marriage to Rupert has been a very good and stabilising influence on my life. We were friends for about two years before we started going out together, so we knew each other very well (and some of the faults) before we started, which I think is very important.

Losing my father I found very difficult to come to terms with. We had always had a rather volatile relationship, but underneath I had always adored him. He had had kidney problems for about two years and had been in and out of hospital, but the end came very suddenly. He died in Scotland in the very severe winter of 1981. We were living in the West Country by then, literally snowed in. It was three weeks before Thomas was due to be born, train services were being delayed by snow and no airline was going to take me and I really couldn't make the 450-mile journey by car. The decision not to get to my father before he died was one of the hardest decisions I have ever had to make and has always left me feeling guilty, but as my doctor kept reminding me, I had to consider the life of my unborn child, and with very high blood-pressure it was not advisable to travel.

When they made *28 Up*, Thomas was two and a half and Oliver about six weeks old. Having children made me grow up and become less selfish. It is a wonderful experience, but also rather frightening when you suddenly realise that you are responsible for another human life.

Suzy at 28, on her marriage:
'I suppose 22 is considered quite young. I felt it was the right time, having found the right person, and don't see what I would have gained by waiting another three years . . . I just felt I was doing the right thing which was extraordinary when only about 18 months before I was very anti it.'

On having children:
'I felt that we'd taken the decision to bring a child into the world and I wanted to bring him up, not somebody else. I feel it's my responsibility to start him off. Whether that will make any difference to how he turns out, I don't know. I just felt I wanted to do it.'

'I don't think I'll have any more. I will get great pleasure from these two but I think I'd want to move on and try something else.'

On boarding school:
'I went to boarding school when I was nine, Rupert went at eight and both of us hated it. I just feel it is too young to send a child off . . . We'd never send the boys off until they are 13.'

On choosing to send her children to private schools:
'I suppose it's what we had, it's what we know.'

Suzy at 28.

On life in the country:
'I had seven years in London and loved most of it, but we'd had enough and much prefer country life.'

On her own childhood:
'. . . as I was growing up I think I was far too sheltered. It's only having grown up that I can appreciate that people are very different, cultures are different.'

On herself at 21:
'I didn't know where I was going at 21, I suppose I thought I was reasonably happy but I had no kind of direction, I obviously hadn't found what I wanted.'

Suzy at 35:

'I think most of us probably changed the most between 21 and 28. I think everybody had done a lot of growing up. I was lucky enough to meet Rupert and he gave me enough confidence to keep going, and I suppose anybody that's happy isn't going to be an insecure wreck.'

My life is very similar to how it was at *28 Up*, except that we are living in a different house and we now have a third child, Laura. I know I said in the previous programme that I wouldn't have any more children but we felt that two was too perfect, like one of those 'cornflake packet' families. Having grown up as more or less an only child, I wanted a bigger family in order to give my children companionship. Although they have their constant fights and ups and downs, I look at them and think, well great, they have the family life that I never had. By the end of the pregnancy, I'd convinced myself that I was going to have three boys, so when Laura was born I nearly fell off the bed. It didn't actually bother Rupert or I whether we had a boy or a girl, I was just so grateful that she had ten fingers and toes and was a healthy baby. You do slightly wonder, having been fortunate enough to have had two healthy children, whether you should push your luck and have another one. You hear these tragic stories and think, why shouldn't it happen to you?

Suzy at 35.

At the moment I very much want to be around the children. Rupert has his own property company which I help out with a little bit, but as the children get older, I would like to spend more time working with him. They are growing up so fast and I love being around to share their daily experiences, although there are some days when I think it would be easier to go back to full-time work, but I know I won't, because when they come home I want them to know that I'll be there and they can talk to me.

Thomas is now nearly nine and goes to a prep school as a day boy, which he really enjoys. They have a long day, not getting home until six o'clock, but at least he still comes home to us in the evening. Most of the children seem to want to be boarders by the age of 11, but that will be up to Thomas, he could stay as a day boy until he leaves at 13. Oliver has co-ordination and learning difficulties and may well be dyslexic, it's too early to tell at the moment. He may not be able to cope in the system he is in at present and will have to move to a school more suited to his needs. Laura is three in two weeks and will be starting nursery school after Christmas. We haven't made any long-term plans for her education but I hope she will guide us as to whether she wants to remain at home or go off to boarding school.

Over the last few months, people have been saying, 'You're nearly 35, are they going to come back to make another programme?' and all the memories, good and bad, come tumbling back, but I think my life is on more of an even keel now than it ever has been. I have my difficult times to get through, but I have Rupert and we are still very happy and all I really want is to bring the children up in a happy family environment.

Suzy and Rupert with their three children, (*left to right*) Oliver, Laura and Thomas.

PAUL

❛ I was going to be a policeman but I thought how hard it would be to join in. ❜

I grew up in London. There was Mum and Dad, Auntie May (I think she owned part of the house we lived in), my older brother Grahame and I. My father was working as a tailor. It was at that time my parents separated. Grahame and I were sent to a children's home in Ashford, Middlesex, and we stayed there for nearly a year, before emigrating to Australia.

I honestly don't have that many memories going back then. I can remember bits and pieces but they're only silly little things, like making our beds in the dormitories and having hot chocolate and buns for supper every now and then. I also remember kids going away on holiday – you used to have to go to the assembly hall and wait for your parents to pick you up. I don't really know how well I got along with other kids at that age. As for interests and hobbies, I was probably keen on sport – English soccer and stuff like that.

Paul at 7, on his life in the children's home:
'Well, I don't like the big boys hitting us and the prefects sending us out for nothing and the monitors up in the washroom sending us out when there's no talking. And I wasn't talking today and Brown sent me out for nothing.'

On fighting:
'I think if someone comes up and starts a fight then I think it serves them right.'

Paul (*left*) and his brother Grahame.

On money:
'I've got 23 threepenny pieces and I don't know how many halfpenny pieces I've got now.'

On marriage:
'. . . say you had a wife, say you had to eat what they cooked you, and say I don't like greens – well I don't – and say she said, "You have to eat what you're give." So I don't like greens, so she gives me greens and . . . that's it.'

On university:
'What does university mean?'

Paul at 35:
'I would say I was unhappy [at the children's home] . . . but I wasn't in there for a long time . . . My father was saying the other day he doesn't even think it was 12 months.'

AT 14

❝ I was going to become a bank accountant but it's more book-taking than maths, and that was the main reason I was thinking about becoming a panel beater . . . I just haven't made up my mind yet. I was going to be a phys. ed. teacher but one of the teachers told me that you had to get up into university. ❞

When I was about seven my dad remarried and took Grahame and I out to Australia. We came out on the ship and my stepmother flew out. I think the first port of call might have been Adelaide but we disembarked in Melbourne.

At first Dad continued working as a tailor. Then after I left school he had a couple of small businesses – a milk bar and a company making pizza boxes.

He ended up as an owner/driver doing deliveries. When we first arrived in Australia he and my stepmother were really busy working, and I think he must have made arrangements for Grahame and me to live in a children's guesthouse in Treemont until he'd established himself.

Grahame was there for three years and I was there for four years, until I was 11. It was a place where you could send your children during the holidays but we stayed there virtually full-time. The people that looked after us, they had two boys and a girl, so we were taken into the family. They had quite a few acres, I'd say, and they used to take us on bush walks and things like that. Those are some of my happiest childhood memories – I had a ball up in the hills and I just really remember those people fondly.

By 14 I was living with my parents and Grahame in Vermont, out in the shadow of the Dandenongs. It was all still being established and there were lots of orchards – 99 per cent orchards where we were. There was a huge area to ramble on. They were happy days.

Around that time I was starting to go horse-riding. I couldn't really ride, I just used to go for fun. And I played football and a bit of cricket – I used to like playing virtually anything. I wasn't a bad swimmer but Grahame was really good. We had a swimming club at high school and I can remember Grahame beating quite a few of them in races.

At high school we had a lot of freedom, but I couldn't handle it. I needed to be told what to do and to make sure that I did it. We were actually told we were guinea-pigs in Form Two. I don't know if it was all that year or just our class, but we were in an experimental era. If there had been someone at that age really standing over me and telling me what to do, who knows how I'd have reacted? I might have got kicked out of school instead of leaving it. I might have really rebelled.

Paul at 14, on his memories of England:
'It seemed to be raining all the time. But I wouldn't stake my life on it because I can't remember very much.'

On his memories of the children's home:
'We didn't mind . . . really because we didn't know what was going on . . . we were a bit young.'

Paul during the filming
of *Seven Plus Seven*.

On sport:

'Basketball appeals to me most . . . With this school I'm one of their best players in Form Two, but when I get into a team they make me look as though I can't play.'

On money:

'Well, out of my permanent jobs I'm getting $4.50.'

On marriage:

'I'd prefer to be alone really. I wouldn't mind living with my brother . . . but otherwise I'd prefer to live alone.'

Paul (*centre*) at 14, in his class photograph.

Paul at 35:

'I know at 14 I would have liked to have been a physical education teacher. That's obviously because of my interest in sport . . . I probably didn't have enough push in me when I was at school. I didn't have that natural ability to push myself and think, "Well, yeah, I can do that," and go for it. My attitude was, "No, I'll never get there . . . I haven't got the brains." I think that's what I used to say to myself.'

AT 21

‘ All I want out of life is to be happy, and when I say happy I want to be happily married. ,

At 16 I'd done Form Four and by all accounts I was struggling. So I decided to leave school and get an apprenticeship in plumbing, electrical work or carpentry, but apprenticeships were fairly hard to get then. Dad thought it was a good idea. He couldn't see me going on too far in school and he thought if I had something on paper, like a trade, that was really important.

In the end I did the bricklaying course at Collingwood Tech. It took three years and we used to go to trade school eight weeks a year in two-week blocks. I didn't mind the schooling but I hated travelling into the city. We had to catch two trains – it would have taken about an hour. That's the most times I've ever caught a train in my life, I'd say.

When I think about it my apprenticeship was actually stretched out to four years. I did three years schooling and one year in the trade, just working on jobs. My first boss was a sub-contractor and there was only him and myself. I was his apprentice on new houses springing up in this area, which suited me because he rarely went towards the city, always away, and I love the bush.

After three years I went to work for another bloke and when I was about 20 I was made a junior partner. I think it's fairly common in the building industry for apprentices to be either made junior partners or to leave their bosses and go out subbing. But I got along pretty well with both bosses, especially the second one, and at that time I didn't see a need to go out completely on my own.

As for the family, Grahame and I were probably reasonably close as far as brothers go, up until about 16. Then he started working and his interests weren't the same as mine for the few years I was still at school. We just slowly grew apart.

Paul and Susan before they were married.

In my free time I used to play football. I went out for a while with a girl whose brother used to play with us. I had a good group of friends and we used to go to a lot of parties. Round about 17 I went through a fairly heavy drinking stage, but I slowed down drastically when I met Sue. I wasn't told to, I just stopped.

I left home at 18 and lived in a place with a mate for a couple of months. Then I moved in with Sue, and we got married just after the *21* show.

Paul at 21, on his memories of the children's home:
'I used to think about running away over that [the golf course]. I was too scared.'

'. . . the boy in the senior part where my brother was, he was sleeping one time and he went out of a second-storey window . . . And we all had to pray for him.'

On his job:
'I'm in bricklaying . . . I enjoy it and it interests me and I'm very content at work.'

On his weaknesses:

'I find it hard to express emotion most of the time, although I'm getting on top of that more now . . . I mean, just the simple things, to say to Susan, you know, "I love you," . . . I really haven't been able to say it freely . . . I suppose that's a weakness.'

On his parents:

'I'm just not that close [to my stepmother]. I'm not really close to my father either.'

Paul at 21.

On himself:

'Everything's started to come good. I've started to enjoy life and I've started to think, "Well, now, I'm not a no-hoper." Because really . . . that's what I've always thought about myself . . . I've always lacked confidence. I still do, to a certain extent, but nothing, nothing like I did, say, when I was 14.'

'. . . now I literally love life, I love people, and I think before I didn't . . . When I was 14 I said . . . something about "I want to be alone." I know even now I meant that. If someone were to drop me out in the Sahara Desert I probably would have been happier, more or less . . . Whereas I'm not like that now. I'd sooner be around people – I don't like doing things by myself. Happiness, to me, is a love for life and a love for people.'

On what he wanted out of life:

'. . . my dreams are all for happiness . . . The houses in Australia, the average sort of living there, will do me fine. It's terrific.'

Paul at 35:

'When I was 21 I said that I didn't feel that close to my dad . . . You know we didn't do a lot of things together . . . and maybe I was looking for a bit more of that side of it . . . That's probably what it was. When I was playing football I could always remember him coming to one match and I thought it would have been nice to have him there a few more times. But that was probably only because I was looking at the other parents being there all the time. Obviously I've always loved my dad.'

' I love the place, you know. I find it hard to put
into words, really, what it is. You've got the
country, you've got bush, outback, you can do
more or less anything you want . . . Whether
you can do that in England, I don't know. '

AT 28

After I'd been made a junior partner it eventually got to the stage where I
ended up asking my boss questions I knew the answer to, and I thought,
'Well, I've got to leave, I'll start using my own head.' It really seemed like a
chance for someone like me to get well and truly ahead, you know, to start
employing people and that. I mean, I didn't want to do it all in one hitch, I
knew I had to build it up slowly. But I just didn't have the business training
and my nature wasn't suited to it. I could get the work, but I didn't know
how to expand on that, how to handle people, how to employ them, that sort
of thing. And I wasn't the sort to say, 'All right, what I don't know I'll learn
from night school.' I didn't think of it that way. I thought I just had to keep
going, but it didn't really work out.

After Sue and I got married we lived in a flat for about three years and
then we saved up and bought a plot of land up in the hills. We wanted to
build a house up there, just doing it on weekends, but we got to the stage
where we started to feel stagnant. It was going to take so long to build the
house and get it finished. We were just getting itchy feet and that's when we
decided to go on a working holiday. So we sold the land and invested the
money to use for buying a house when we came back.

We were planning to have a family but we expected it would take a fair
while for Sue to get pregnant. The original aim was to go all around Australia
but we've always been fairly practical. We just decided we'd come back
whenever Susan was uncomfortable and wanted to come home, whether it
was six months, 12 months or two years. In the end we were away for seven
months. We saw a lot of Western Australia and a fair bit of the Northern
Territory, although we travelled fairly slowly.

At first we stayed with Sue's sister in Swan Hill and worked there for about
three weeks. Then we started to drive across the Nullarbor and stopped in a
place called Esperance for about a month. When we started the trip I said I'd
take any work except bricklaying and Sue said she'd do anything except her

Paul at 28.

usual job, which was hairdressing. Of course, I ended up doing nothing but bricklaying and Sue did nothing but hairdressing! It would have been really good experience to do other things but it was so easy to get work in our own trade and the money was better. We had an absolute ball but I just wish we'd done other things, for the experience. I'd really love to have been a jackaroo on a sheep station. I think that would have been great.

We found out in Carnarvon that Susan was pregnant but we kept travelling up to Darwin. We thought we'd just keep going and come back down the centre, but then we started wanting to get back for Christmas, and we knew we had to find a house.

When we came back we had enough for a deposit on a house and we started looking. We must have looked at 52 houses and we couldn't make up our minds. Then we found this place. It was nothing spectacular but it was what we were looking for. We moved in about six weeks before Katie was born. And then Robert was born a year later. He was 11 months old when they made the *28* programme.

We got back from our trip at Christmas and a lot of builders here go on holiday so it was pretty hard to get back to sub-contracting at first. For a while I worked with a friend of mine, a carpenter, but there wasn't the continuity of work because everywhere was closed down. After that I worked for another bloke for about three months and then I went back out subbing.

Paul at 28, on trying to expand his business:
'If you're talking about employing other people, I'm not hard enough.'

On his family:
'We're Mr and Mrs Average, this is true. You know, we probably earn an average income, just an average family.'

Paul and Susan.

On what he wanted for his children:
'A happier family life [than I had] . . . Don't get me wrong – I wasn't miserable – but I think it could have been better. I think that would be one of the most important things.'

'But it would be nice to let them go one step up from us, I think . . . Put it this way, I hope he's better at schoolwork than I was, so that he's got a choice. Because, really, the educational standard I got, I didn't have a choice.'

On education:

'I didn't work hard enough. I was just very lazy at school. You know, if you're lazy and you don't work at school you suffer for it. There needs to be a little more discipline.'

'If private schools are better, you'd be far better off spending your money sending your kids there than getting a video or a new television, swimming pool or something like that.'

On his father:

'We were sort of distant friends and . . . we always got along fairly well. We didn't see much of each other.'

On divorce:

'Divorcing your wife, what does it get you? It messes up your own life, it messes up the kids' lives, wife's life. I don't think half the people that get divorced even think about it properly.'

On the influence of his parents' divorce:

'The only thing I can say that I think might have come from that is just my lack of confidence and being able to show my feelings.'

On himself at 7:

'I suppose you could see me now when I was seven in a way. I think it was pretty obvious I wasn't going to be a doctor.'

'I was pretty . . . long-faced. I was like that sometimes out here too – I was always getting knocked about.'

On his life in Australia:

'We've got a lot more than what we would have had in England, from what other people tell us. But there again, when it comes to work, I don't sit down on my backside, I'll go and chase it. So it's hard to say . . . In general, I've probably done better here than what I would have done there.'

On his future:

'The family's going to come first but I'll still be working. And we'll progress, you know.'

AT 35

Paul at 35.

I was working as a sub-contractor up until about three years ago. Then I went into partnership with a carpenter, building extensions and new homes. The original job was to learn to be a supervisor but that didn't last very long, then the offer was that they were going to teach me carpentry. To me, carpentry is a real thinking-man's trade and I think it would have done me the world of good. I was really keen on learning that, but, unfortunately for me, my partner was in a sort of transition stage himself and he decided to try other things.

We stuck together and went into maintenance, doing anything from underpinning and brick blocking to hanging doors. We used to have to tackle jobs that other places would sooner not do and I was virtually like an apprentice again, standing behind my partner and saying, 'OK, what do we do now?'

When I left bricklaying and started in the partnership I thought it was my big chance. I just felt I had so much to learn and I was really fired up to it. But then I started worrying too much about what everyone else would think of my work, and I felt I'd somehow lost control of the situation. It was a bit of a disappointment.

Last year my partner decided he wanted to go small again – he didn't want the headaches – and I started work for a plant hire company, renting out all sorts of building equipment. We did machinery, electrical equipment, wheelbarrows, planks, trestles, rollers – you name it. It was all so foreign to me, because I had to do the maintenance on the equipment and I'd never had to use complicated equipment in bricklaying. Even driving the truck around, doing the deliveries, it worried the heck out of me whether I'd be able to cope with it.

Now I'm working with my former partner again, and we specialise in underpinning foundations. We've mainly been doing domestic work on brick veneer homes, and up until a short while ago we had heaps of work. It was a good way to earn good money with less headaches than in building extensions. But it's slowed down a hell of a lot now. Fortunately we've got a backlog up to Christmas so hopefully we'll pick more work up before then.

When I first worked with my partner he knew I was desperate to get out of bricklaying, because I literally got tired of it and I couldn't see it going anywhere. And he said, 'Come with me, boy, you won't ever have to lay another brick.' And right from the word go, the first job we were on, I was laying bricks. It's just the way things turned out – I had to keep laying bricks on and off. And this time, when I left the plant hire firm and he offered me the job to go back working for him, he said, 'Well, I know how much you hate laying bricks, so we'll use subbies to do any of our repair work that's incorporated in the underpinning.' But again it didn't take long. Australia's economic situation won't allow for him to use subbies at the moment. It's better for us, it's kept us working on one job longer. I've never really been able to get away from bricklaying completely.

Before I started work in the partnership the first time, Sue and I felt like we'd just got on our feet. We were in this house and everything was starting to come together. Then we borrowed a bit of money for the business and it unsettled us – I had to take lower wages and work longer hours. It's only been in the last 12 months that we've started feeling we've got back to the position we were in before, three years ago.

I'm glad I went into the partnership but my attitude's changed. It's not that I don't want to improve my situation and earn more money but it's not something that's worrying me. Jobwise, I suppose I wish I'd finished my apprenticeship and tried something else – not just one job, several jobs to get more experience in other things – which I think would have helped my confidence grow a bit. But right at this moment I can't think of much else I'd change.

We live in a three-bedroomed house, with a nice car in the garage, and everything's coming together nicely. Rob's now seven and Katie's eight. It sort of surprised me, the way I felt about becoming a father, because I'd always liked other people's kids but I'd kept my distance from them. I never used to hold babies or anything like that, and I always wondered what I was going to be like when I had my own. You hear a lot of fathers say this, but I couldn't believe my reaction when they were born – I just broke down. And now I've changed a little bit even towards other people's kids, I'm more forward with them.

I suppose Susan does about 90 per cent when it comes to looking after the kids. She's really good, she does a hell of a lot at the school. I try to give her some support – I take Katie to dancing sometimes and Rob to football – but obviously not as much as I'd like. The schools round here are pretty good. The approach to children is a bit different from when I was at school but we're fairly happy.

Paul and Susan.

Paul and Susan with Katie and Robert.

I've always got along well with my dad, despite how it may have appeared in the past. We see a fair bit of him. He was here yesterday and we call him two or three times a week. It's a pretty normal father/son relationship really.

I would like to do a lot more riding, but at this time I am limited to the odd occasion, going for one four-day ride a year. About six years ago a friend of mine did some rides in the high country about two and a half hours out of Melbourne. He really enjoyed himself and he came round and started talking to me about it. I told him I'd had an interest in riding when I was about 14 but I could never really ride then. He was telling me about going through paddocks and jumping over sheep, going along narrow trails with sheer drops on the side, and having to jump logs that were over the tracks. He was on at me for six months to go on a three-day ride and in the end Susan wrote out a cheque for $25 deposit and said, 'He wants to go, he just can't make up his mind!' So I ended up going and I loved it.

The people that ran the place, they all said, 'Don't worry, by the end of the three days you'll be right.' The first half-day I thought, 'God, I've got two and a half more days of this.' I didn't think I'd be able to cope, but by the end of the first day I was a lot happier. I enjoyed sitting round the campfires at night and I just had a ball.

At the moment I think Sue and I are pretty contented. We're starting to worry less about silly things, little problems and that. You know, you work at them but you don't worry about them. I don't try to plan my life that much, but being in the show I reckon subconsciously it makes you analyse yourself a bit more, which I don't like to do.

Until recently, living in Australia, not too many people had seen the show, so I literally forgot about it. But it was shown here on SBS twice and because of that you get quite a few people talking to you about it. Don't get me wrong, I haven't had crowds of people coming up to me, but some people have just wanted to talk about it at the wrong time and you think, 'Oh, not again.' Nearly everyone who's spoken to me has been really nice about it, but I'm not really the sort that wants to be recognised.

What would I like to be doing in another seven years? I suppose ideally I'd like to move a little bit further out of Melbourne, but that may not be possible. It's not a hate of the city as much as I just really love the country, the bush. And it doesn't have to be bush and forest, I even like the completely barren landscapes. There's just something about it – I've never known how to put it in words.

I am apprehensive about moving to a country area because I just don't know how it would go. We've always been a bit worried about finding work. A lot of people have said to us that you've virtually got to be a policeman or a nurse to leave the city for the bush and stay there for the rest of your life, because if things go wrong, you run out of work and have to move back. I'd hate to go to a country town and not get along with people. That would be terrible. But then you shouldn't really worry about that, should you? You should just go for it.

HOW TO MAKE YOUR OWN SEVEN UP

Precious moments of childhood captured with a still camera have always filled the pages of family albums. In many families the photograph album is their most treasured possession. Today, with the development of cheaper, more user-friendly video cameras and camcorders, it's possible to take that family album a stage further.

Increasing familiarity with new technology means that, with a little practice, even a novice film-maker can quite quickly build up their own walking, talking family album. To help you make your own Seven Up, here are some suggestions which should smooth the way to reasonable proficiency in camerawork, directing and interviewing.

INTERVIEWING

General tips

- Six to seven is the best age to start the first interviews.

- It is much better to get someone who is *not* a member of the close family to interview the child. If the parent or relative is operating the camera, make sure the child understands that he or she is so busy filming they can't take part. Parents tend to inhibit children's answers.

- The interviewer needs to be completely detached and no comments should be made about any of the child's replies. The child should be told at the beginning that there are no right or wrong answers.

- Don't overtire children when interviewing. Stop and rest if they become fidgety.

- If they appear nervous tell them you are just practising.

- Sometimes children are more comfortable when interviewed with a friend – and it often produces hilarious results!

- Above all, make the interview fun.

- As well as interviewing children, use the camera to record them at certain favourite activities. This helps to date the period.

- Keep a careful note of the questions you ask at seven. Remember, you'll never have another chance so it's better to film too much than too little.

- When you make follow-up films at 14 and 21 try, if possible, to use the same interviewer – this will give consistency to the questions and make the 'child' feel more at home.

Questions

- Work out a list of questions covering topics which are important to the child, such as school, family and home, hobbies and interests, boyfriends or girlfriends, career ambitions, current crazes, likes and dislikes, and TV. Other key areas to ask about are fighting and violence, dreams and nightmares, marriage, politics and world affairs. The child's own interests may give you other ideas for questions.

- The key to good interviewing is to get the child to talk, that is to *describe*. 'Tell me', 'Why' and 'How' are all very helpful ways to begin your questions.

- Try to avoid questions which allow the child to answer 'Yes' or 'No' – or they will! For instance:
  Question: Do you like school?
  Probable answer: No.
  Better question: Tell me about your school.
  Then: Do you like it?
  Probable answer: No.
  Question: Why not?

- Try to listen to the child's replies and ask good follow-up questions rather than just asking questions from your list.

For instance:

Question: Who lives in your house with you?

Answer: Mum, Gran, my brothers.

Bad next question: What kind of house is it?

Better next question: Does your dad live with you? *or* Tell me about it.

FILMING

George Jesse Turner, cameraman on *21 Up, 28 Up* and *35 Up*.

George Jesse Turner, award-winning *World in Action* cameraman, and cameraman on *21 Up*, *28 Up* and *35 Up* says:

'The biggest thing for anybody to learn is to hold the camera still and let the action take place within the frame. There's a great temptation for most amateur cameramen to pan it up and down buildings and when you come to show it to the in-laws or friends it actually looks pretty dreadful because the camera's never been still long enough! Surprisingly, if you hold the camera still for a length of time, even just looking down a street, there'll be life passing by there that actually happens naturally within the frame so that when somebody's looking at it they can digest it at their own leisure.

'I'm a great believer, maybe because of the documentaries that I've made over the years, in trying to catch people as naturally as possible, so hopefully you're not going to get them ''acting'' in front of the camera all the time. What that means is stepping *back* and *observing* from maybe two paces further back than you feel you should.

'The other thing, with a lot of these new video cameras, is you can put them on to an automatic iris and automatic focus and they zoom in and out. However, if you pan a bit to follow the action, the focus starts to ''hunt'' and can register something that's a bit nearer but which isn't important. The secret is just to learn to hold the camera still.'

Michael Apted says:

'Keep it simple and don't give up on it. Even if sometimes the answers and pictures don't feel inspired now, over the years they will be richer – an invaluable record of your child.'